GREEN SPACE IN THE COMMUNITY

Edited by Steffan Robel

images
Publishing

Contents

Preface

Steffan Robel
Founder and executive director A24 Landschaft

The urbanization of society is a path of unbroken progress. In 2014 a threshold was surpassed: more humans now live in cities than in rural areas.[1] In spite of this fact, or because of it, the urban population's longing for open areas and nature in close proximity to their homes is growing. This is not an entirely new phenomenon. Industrialization in the middle of the nineteenth century awakened efforts to reverse the trend of alienation towards nature. The creation of Europe's first Volksparks (literally, "people's parks") at the start of the twentieth century began a transformation of stately urban civic parks into usable green space. The new parks performed a hygiene function and health and social role, providing fresh air and light and an open area for human interaction and fitness.

The fundamental ambitions for public green space have not since changed in any significant way. People still desire a mix of leisure, recreation, sports, and culture. However, as our society has grown more diverse, the ideas of how to fulfill these desires have become more individualized. Today's parks now encompass sports facilities ranging from skatepools to beach volleyball courts, and they must be flexible and adaptive–hybrid spaces between nature and culture.

Two additional and essential requirements have come to the fore, beyond this pluralistic aspect. One is the amplified imperative to embrace ecological functions, be they open areas for climatic adjustment in cities, water filtration, water management or, for example, water collection as in "The Source" park in Zeist in the Netherlands. The growth of Zeist has led to its groundwater catchment area to now be situated within the community, rather than in the open countryside where it once was. The aspiration to augment classical recreational elements with "green engineering" has resulted in the idea of the "smart city" being integrated into parks. Smart cities utilize new technologies, such as eco-engineering, and undergo smart maintenance management by way of networks and public contribution to the benefit of the city and society.

This leads to the second new requirement: the conscious participation of citizens. For quite some time the life of modern city dwellers has evolved not only in their own homes but also, increasingly, outside of their homes. The migration of the private sphere towards the public sphere has been paralleled by the desire and will for co-design and participation. Furthermore, municipalities, urban planners, and landscape architects have recognized that distinct neighborhoods' individual requirements for outdoor public space can often best be realized through open dialogue. Two projects in this book exemplify how essential civic participation is to the planning process: The Community-based Reinvention of Teleki Square in Budapest, Hungary, and Catene's Public Park in Marghera, Venice.

This publication presents a multitude of ways to design green space for the Community. While showing a wide variation of possibilities, these projects are united by the inclusion of nature and landscape in an urban environment. Munich's Parkstadt Schwabing echoes the panorama of the nearby Bavarian Alps. Water Collection Park "The Source", adapts an infrastructure function in the center of town. The abstract and artificial landscape of Mary Bartelme Park, on the grounds of a former hospital in Chicago, Illinois, is a complex topography that offers a diverse range of play areas in a busy neighborhood. Under markedly unnatural preconditions, Catharina Amalia Park, a formerly lost landscape element in Netherlands' Apeldoorn, is now reactivated as a stream and rerouted to flow above an underground garage. Catene's Public Park in Marghera, Venice, has been integrated into the typical landscape elements of the region while utilizing the existing water and tree structures. The historical use of a landscape is referenced in Neisse Waterfront Park, in Görlitz, Germany, where the configuration of paths along the river bank recalls the former textile industry and the lengths of cloth laid out for bleaching. The new Bürgerpark Paunsdorf is situated between a residential neighborhood, trade fair grounds, and industrial locations, and serves as a landscaped frame of reference for a group of very heterogeneous urban elements. In contrast, Conversion Estienne-et-Foch Barrack in Landau, Germany, conducts a dialogue between cultural landscape and natural landscape.

This brief overview of a portion of the projects curated for this book underscores the diversity of interesting aspects inherent to this theme. Green space invigorates our communities, and forms vital centers of a diverse society. Enjoy your reading.

1. United Nations, Department of Economic and Social Affairs, Population Division, "Population Facts: Our Urbanizing World," no. 2014/03, August 2014, 1, accessed January 2016, http://www.un.org/en/development/desa/population/publications/pdf/popfacts/PopFacts_2014-3.pdf

Introduction

Now, more than ever before, people across the world are living in urban areas. Indeed, as of 2010 more than half of the world population lives in cities, which are consequently growing in both size and number (Cities Alliance 2010). This inevitably brings huge challenges around how to develop a sustainable infrastructure for these global cities.

Public green space within cities—parks, gardens, squares, streets, and cemeteries—are an often overlooked component of this sustainable infrastructure and international comparisons indicate a huge variation in how much area is given over to green space in world cities (BOP Consulting 2013). As Table 1 shows, Singapore is the greenest world city with nearly 50 percent of its surface area consisting of green space.

This poses the question: why is green space important in the community? This is harder to answer than, for example, identifying the benefits of housing or transport. However, in a context where pressure on urban land use is only going to intensify and people live increasingly removed from nature, it is a question that needs to be answered (BOP Consulting 2013). Therefore this book sets out to investigate the importance of sustainable and well-designed green space in urban communities.

Successful Green Space

Green space in the community is an area of open ground that is partly or completely covered with grass, trees, shrubs, or vegetation, and available for recreational use. Indeed successful green space is not only accessible; it is engaging, comfortable, attractive, functional, and safe. Thus successful green space should meet the following requirements:

· Be located at the center of a neighborhood, or intersection of neighborhoods, where it can serve a large community or several small communities.

· Be close to nearby urban arteries and transport hubs, and be linked with walking and bicycle lanes.

· Serve the relevant needs of community residents.

· Provide recreation and leisure facilities.

· Provide green area that occupies more than 50 percent of the total size of the space.

The design of green space should also promote diverse activity across a range of user groups, and be responsive to their changing needs during the course of a day and over changing seasons. As such, successful green space should include the following features:

· A rich and varied environment that conveys a "natural" appearance and encourages contact with nature.

· A planning process that engages the local community in the design, maintenance, and care of the green space.

· Spaces designed to cater for a variety of activity.

· Activity areas defined by trees and other planting to mark and buffer spaces.

· Spaces and furnishings that present opportunities for passive and active socializing.

· Seating located and designed for users of all abilities and disabilities, with attention to climate and orientation.

· Provisions and furniture (e.g. picnic tables) for group activities.

· Good connectivity to the surrounding community with multiple entry/exit points.

· A circulation system that allows users to move through the green space safely, easily, and conveniently.

· Pathways of different lengths to encourage physical movement.

· Activity generators (e.g. chessboard tables) within seating areas or alongside pedestrian pathways.

· Open visual access into and through the green space.

· A diversified local habitat (Open Space in Medium-density Housing Guidelines for Planning and Design 2013).

This book explores green space around the world that meets these requirements and incorporates these features. These spaces range

Table 1. World cities' public green space by proportion of surface area, 2012.

City	Figure (%)
Singapore	47
Sydney	46
London	38.4
Johannesburg-Gauteng	24
Berlin	14.4
New York	14
Paris	9.4
Tokyo	3.44
Shanghai	2.6
Mumbai	2.5
Istanbul	1.5

*Source: World Cities Culture Report, BOP 2012, cited in BOP Consulting 2013.

in type, and each is planned and designed to cater to the needs of diverse user groups.

Types of Green Space

Green space can be classified into various types or typologies according to its function, use, size, and facilities. Table 2 summarizes the types of green space that can be found in urban communities.

User Groups of Green Space

It is of great importance to assess the demographic, cultural, and lifestyle preferences of the local community when planning and designing green space. This assessment should pose questions such as: will children, elderly, or people from different cultures use the park? Are residents seeking fitness opportunities or a space to rest and socialize? Will users walk, drive, cycle, or take public transport to the park? The answers will contribute towards the planning and design of the green space. Table 3 summarizes the specific needs

particular user groups may have for green space and that should be considered in the process of planning and design.

Role and Benefits of Green Space

Green space plays a variety of roles in contributing to the sustainability of the environment and a higher standard of living. Green space can facilitate social interaction and improved physical and mental health, as well as enhancing the attractiveness of the environment, aiding cooling of urban areas, and supporting natural systems. It can also improve property values while decreasing government costs. The following benefits of public green space are adapted from the 2013 report *Green Spaces: The Benefits for London*, prepared for the City of London Corporation, and are based on the BOP Consulting's literature review of international evidence.

Table 2. Types of green space in urban communities

Type of Green Space	Description	Additional notes
Pocket park	A small area, such as a city block, meeting limited recreational needs. Typically has seating and a children's play area, and natural features such as grass and trees.	It provides proximity to home, which is especially important for children and older people with less mobility or territorial range.
Neighborhood park	A larger area that provides space for active and passive recreational activities and social interactions. Facilities may include play equipment, picnic tables, and green space, and some limited sporting facilities. Natural features include grassed areas and shade planting.	It should support diverse activity in order to meet users' needs; it should not be dominated by sporting fields.
Roof garden	A roof garden can serve the same function as a pocket park, however it is located on the rooftop of an apartment building or similar. It can provide some recreational areas and may include play or fitness equipment. It offers visual relief, habitat protection, and cooling effects, and can also be used to grow food.	Care needs to be taken for all planning due to the elevated height of the roof garden. Vertical green walls can add to its atmosphere and environmental benefits.
Privately controlled spaces offering public access	A privately owned and/or managed green space may offer the public access to places such as schools, churches, or sports club facilities. Typically includes playing fields and/or courts.	These spaces should only be relied on as public space if their long-term accessibility can be guaranteed. Access may need to be renegotiated if the facility is sold or a change in personnel occurs. Other potential obstacles include insurance and indemnity issues, and restricted hours of use.
Green connector, or green street	A green connector is a linear corridor that provides an area for pedestrians, cyclists, joggers, dog walkers, and others, to navigate a section of an urban area with uninterrupted access (i.e., with no or limited vehicular traffic). It may include traffic-calming elements, wider sidewalks, shaded seating, and landscaped areas.	These may be viewed as transitory spaces rather than destinations, providing improved access to other urban areas.
Linear park	A linear park is substantially longer than it is wide and is often built on public strips of land or waterway, or over disused transport corridors. It often contributes to a pedestrian or cycle network for improved access in and through an urban area.	These serve as both transition spaces and destinations, offering the amenity of a neighborhood park and green connector.

Adapted from the table compiled by Andrea Young. Source: Sarkissian, Bateman, Hurley, and Young 2013.

Table 3. Green space needs of specific community resident groups

Resident Characteristics	Behavior or activity to be supported	Facilities, furnishing, and programming
Households with children		
	Preschool children's play	Shaded and safe playground equipment, nearby restroom and drinking fountain, and lighting, especially near toilets, for safe and comfortable play.
	School children's play	Slides, climbing walls, and other challenging playground equipment for school children aged six years of age and over; playground equipment that incorporates nature.
	Adult supervision of children's play	Comfortable and shaded seating close to play areas for clear views of the entire play area.
	Organized physical group activity	Fixtures such as a basketball hoop, tennis practice wall, football goal, or baseball diamond for structured games, sports, and activities.
	Individual physical activity	Lawn, path, track, or similar for running, or throwing and kicking a ball.
	Barbecuing and picnicking	Barbecue facilities and picnic tables close to children's play area for outdoor dining and supervision.
	Adults pushing children and infants in strollers	Wide and level paths for safe and convenient use of prams and strollers.
Teenagers		
	Space to socialize with friends	Informal and natural spaces for socializing with peers away from other activities or adult interference. Discrete spaces with planned and unplanned seating fixtures, such as benches or steps, for sitting and meeting with friends. Facilities such as skate parks, basketball goals, practice courts, and performance spaces to encourage physical activity.
Adults		
	Casual social encounters and relaxed social activities	Expansive lawn area with some shaded areas for a variety of casual outdoor activities, such as sunbathing, sleeping, reading, picnicking, chatting, lawn bowls, bocce ball, or tossing a Frisbee. Paved areas with shaded/covered perimeter seating for socializing, outdoor dining, sitting, or activities such as playing chess.
	Entertainment	Stage/amphitheater for casual or programmed performances.
	Picnicking, barbecuing, and entertaining	Barbecue facilities and picnic tables for outdoor dining.
	Exercise	Trails and/or circuits for walking/jogging/cycling and other exercise. Tennis and/or other hard-surfaced courts for games and sports.
	Bicycling	Bicycle parking with good visibility from all areas of the space for safe and accessible bicycle storage.
	Socializing in twos and threes	Benches and other seating for conversation and social interaction.
	Seeking solace	Seating off the main path or circuit for relaxation. Seating on the main path or circuit for people watching and being seen. Promenade area with spatial designs for culturally and socially specific interactions; for example, some cultures traditionally prefer paved plazas while others prefer natural landscapes. Seating in solitary locations that are perceived as safe and private. Pathways with different sensory experiences, such as views, flora, or fauna, for pleasant walking or movement.
	Unforced social encounters to combat isolation, shyness, and/or loneliness	Areas of interesting and attractive vegetation and shaded and/or covered seating near green space entrances for socializing and accommodating those who do not wish to venture further into the green space.
	Walking	Clearly marked pathways through the green space for easy wayfinding. Seats and benches for sitting when needed. Safe and smooth pathways around the perimeter of the green space for circuit walking. Handrails for those who need balance support.
People with disabilities		
	Universal access	Continuous pathway into and within the green space for safer and convenient access and passage. Ramps in place of steps, stairs, or other impediments, and handrails where necessary for safe and convenient access and passage. Paths wide enough for two wheelchairs to pass. Table and seating arrangements for accommodating wheelchairs.

Adapted from the table compiled by Andrea Young. Source: Sarkissian, Bateman, Hurley, and Young 2013.

Environmental Role and Benefits

Green space can offer ecological support for biodiversity, species migration, and urban repair. Climate-responsive design, as illustrated in Figure 1, can counteract localized warming due to the heat island effect, helping to cool and ventilate dense urban development, along with mitigating greenhouse gas emissions through carbon sequestration. Green space can also play an important role in attenuating floodwaters and assisting food security as community gardens can offer local residents opportunities to grow their own food. Environmental benefits of green space in the community include:

Cooler Air and Less Heat Retention

Across the world, metropolitan areas are significantly warmer than their surrounding areas. This is due to urban surfaces being constructed with materials that retain heat, such as brick and concrete, as well as high levels of energy usage that waste heat in cities. This effect may be intensified in the context of global warming. Green space mitigates this effect by providing an open and natural area that provides shade during the day.

In 2010 Forest Research published *Benefits of Green Infrastructure. Report to Defra and CLG*. The results of it systematic review of a range of studies investigating temperatures within and outside urban parks determined that studies were generally consistent in finding lower surface temperatures in green space than in built-up space. An analysis of the temperatures put forward by the various studies showed average temperature reductions in green space to be just below 1.8°F (1°C) during the day and 2.07°F (1.15°C) at night. The authors of the review concluded the research clearly points toward the potential of green space to reduce urban air temperature (Bowler et al. 2010).

Contributing to these findings, a 2005 study of two parks in Singapore found average temperatures to be lower inside the parks, and becoming warmer with increasing distance from the parks. The authors thus concluded the importance of large city green space for decreasing urban heat (Yu and Hien 2005). In 2007, a wide-ranging study of 61 city parks in Taipei came to the same conclusion, finding urban parks to be on average cooler than their surroundings. The researchers also found larger parks to be on average cooler than smaller ones (though the relationship was non-linear), and that park characteristics, such as the types of vegetation and size of natural versus non-natural areas, also influenced the level of impact on temperature (Chang, Li, and Chang 2007).

Reduced Stormwater Runoff and Improved Water Quality

Stormwater runoff refers to water flowing over the land during and immediately following a rainstorm. Urban surface materials are more prone to causing flooding than natural surface materials due to their impermeable quality. Indeed, Forest Research found much of the floods in England in 2000 to be caused by impenetrable urban surfaces exacerbated by failing urban drainage systems. This problem is worsened by the fact that urban flooding is frequently polluted. In addition, climate change is predicted to increase the risk of flooding in the future—a tendency that already seems visible. In contrast, green infrastructure provides natural drainage, water interception, infiltration, and storage of stormwater, which contribute to a reduction in surface flow and flood alleviation. It also removes pollutants from soil and water, resulting in better water quality.

In 2012, researchers in China claimed that only a few studies to date have explored the benefits of urban green space in reducing stormwater runoff. However, one frequently cited study from 1999 concluded lawns, parks, urban forests, cultivated lands, and wetlands in Stockholm provided an important contribution to the city's drainage system (Bolund and Hunhammar 1999, cited in Forest Research 2010). The study explained this is due to soft ground allowing water to seep through rather than runoff, and vegetation storing and releasing water through evapotranspiration (Bolund and Hunhammar 1999, cited in Zhang et al. 2012).

Supporting this finding, the 2012 Chinese study analyzed the stormwater runoff potential of all green space in Beijing. It

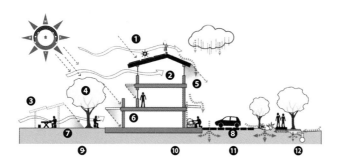

① Harness elements where possible
② Capture cooling breezes
③ Artificial shade structures
④ Trees make excellent shade structures
⑤ Building walls effectively shade, but can also darken spaces
⑥ Assist shading with structures
⑦ Capture cooling breezes
⑧ Permeable paving
⑨ Passive shading cools open spaces and buildings
⑩ Capture stormwater water for gardening
⑪ Promote designs for stormwater retention and infiltration
⑫ Integrate natural systems and public infrastructure

Figure 1. Climate-responsive design © Brendan Hurley

estimated the green space stored a total volume of 5.44 billion cubic feet (154 million cubic meters) of stormwater, reducing potential runoff by 10,864 cubic feet per acre (2,494 cubic meters per hectare) of green area (Zhang et al. 2012).

Similarly, researchers in the UK developed a 2080 surface runoff model for Greater Manchester and suggested a 10 percent increase in green ground cover in residential areas could reduce runoff by 4.9 percent, and a 10 percent increase in tree cover could cause a further reduction of 5.7 percent (Gill et al. 2007).

Other research in Beijing analyzed the quality of water collected in green space and found the water stored in green areas to be superior in quality to the runoff from roofs and roads, thus reducing purification costs (Hou 2006, cited in Zhang et al. 2012).

Improved Air Quality

Cities are pollution hotspots due to the increased concentration of vehicle emissions, power production, industrial activity, and aviation. Pollution not only causes damage to a city's built and natural environment, but can also aggravate cardiovascular and respiratory diseases among urban populations. Green infrastructure has the ability to absorb pollutants, helping to improve air quality.

In 2013, a systematic review concluded there is currently only relatively weak evidence that urban parks improve air quality by capturing pollutants and particles. This is because most existing studies that look at the contribution of urban green space to air quality rely on modeling rather than empirical research (Konijnendijk et al. 2013).

However, Forest Research's 2010 review of the benefits of green infrastructure is considerably more definitive, concluding trees can directly alter air quality through their capacity to absorb gaseous pollutants, intercept particles at leaf surface, and produce oxygen during photosynthesis.

The review cites a number of studies providing evidence to this effect. A 1994 study found trees in Chicago removed an estimated 6,190 tons (5.6 million kilograms) of pollution per year—an average improvement in air quality of approximately 0.3 percent—with the possibility of a further 5 to 10 percent improvement to air quality through increased tree cover (Nowak 1994, cited in Forest Research 2010). In 2009, researchers in London based their study on an area of the East London Green Grid measuring 6.2 miles by 6.2 miles (10 kilometers by 10 kilometers) and demonstrated the potential for green space to reduce particulate pollution (PM10) (Tiwary et al. 2009, cited in Forest Research 2010). Research undertaken in China provided similar results. Researchers assessed the impact of urban

vegetation on air pollution in Guangzhou with results indicating the removal of sulfur dioxide, nitrogen dioxide, and total suspended particulates of about 0.01 ounces (312.03 milligrams) annually (Jim and Chen 2007).

While the strength of the evidence base is contested, many authors nevertheless conclude their reports by suggesting tree planting as a cost-effective measure to reduce different types of air pollution (Jim and Chen 2007 and Tiwary et al. 2009, cited in Forest Research 2010). This indicates there is certainly some consensus with regard to the role green space can play in reducing pollution.

Climate Change Mitigation

Carbon emissions—again a particular problem in big cities—have been linked to increasing global warming. Similar to pollution, urban green infrastructure and trees enable carbon capture and sequestration, thereby mitigating emissions and their negative effects, and the broader context of climate change.

To date, little high-profile research exists specifically on the effects of urban green space on carbon capture. However, studies that more generally look at the link between green space and pollution often list carbon capture alongside the capacity of green space for pollution reduction and particle absorption.

The 2009 report *Combating Climate Change–A Role for UK Forests*, prepared for the National Assessment of UK Forestry and Climate Change Steering Group, looked more specifically at carbon capture and concluded UK forests and trees have a significant role to play in the country's response to the challenges posed by climate change. Indeed, the report claims a 4 percent increase in woodland in the UK could deliver annual emissions abatement equivalent to 10 percent of total greenhouse gas emissions (Read et al. 2009).

While this study does not specifically mention urban vegetation (although it includes trees generally), Forest Research's 2010 report drew on this study to conclude that urban green infrastructure also contributes to carbon capture by, for example, building up soil carbon reserves over time.

Improved Biodiversity and Ecosystem Health

A city's built-up urban area offers only very limited space for wildlife. In contrast, a city's green infrastructure can provide a suitable environment for various species and a "green network"—a series of connected green spaces—can afford opportunities for animals and insects to move, spread, and colonize new habitats.

A number of research reviews claim that, while sound in theory, there is little evidence of the overall value of green space for all species. While many studies have researched wildlife within urban areas they frequently consider only a particular species' use of green space. For example, Forest Research lists studies that looked specifically at the number of deer, badgers, and foxes in urban areas (by counting vehicle collisions), at insect populations in urban roundabouts, and at birds' use of urban green infrastructure.

While such studies provide evidence that certain types of animals or insects use urban green space, they offer more limited evidence of the value of urban green networks on wildlife as a whole (and, as such, on biodiversity). However, as one study points out, action to provide urban green networks as "conduits for wildlife" nevertheless often takes place due to an absence of alternatives, and "ecological networks" have thus become a popular element of urban planning (Haddad and Tewsbury 2005 and Jongman and Pungetti 2004, cited in Tzoulas et al. 2007).

Health and Well-being Role and Benefits

The greater the proximity and more direct the route of a home to a green space, the greater the likelihood of physical activity. As such, green space should be within walking distance of residences and well linked to other spaces using green connectors, linear parks, and cycling and walking trails to encourage physical activity.

Nature has restorative qualities that can have beneficial effects on human health and well-being; indeed even a view of a green space from a house or apartment window can contribute positively to a person's mental health. Access to nature can provide both psychological and spiritual benefits, such as relaxation, social interaction, or moderated exposure to the sun. It can also help children and adults develop ecological awareness and environmental responsibility. Health and well-being benefits of green space include:

Improved Physical Health

Poor air quality, urban heat, and an increasingly "sedentary lifestyle" among today's urban population are frequently linked to problems of ill health (Shah and Peck 2005). In particular, they have been found to contribute to cardiovascular and respiratory diseases and increased levels of obesity in adults and children. Green space can help to counteract such health problems by improving air quality and providing areas for physical exercise.

A 2011 literature review for NHS Ashton, Leigh and Wigan cites a number of studies from the past ten that have found links between urban green space and improved physical health among the local population. These studies focused on indications of reduced obesity, reduced risk of coronary heart disease and strokes, decreased blood pressure, lower cholesterol, and better overall perceived health (Richardson and Parker 2011).

A large-scale UK study of patient records in 2008 is one such analysis. It found mortality from circulatory diseases due to income deprivation-related health inequalities to be lower among residents in the greenest areas. Controlling for other factors that may be associated with mortality, as well as for characteristics of certain areas, the authors concluded that access to green space helps reduce health inequalities in regard to circulatory diseases (Mitchell and Popham 2008).

Studies most commonly link such health benefits to the capacity of green space to promote physical activity. However, reviews looking at links between the two vary in their assertiveness. One study concluded the amount of green space in peoples' living environment is not related to them meeting health recommendations for physical activity (Maas et al. 2008, cited in Richardson and Parker 2011). Similarly, another claimed the existence of a causal relationship between green space and physical activity as still uncertain, even though it is based on strong theory and supported by a large amount of observational evidence (Mytton et al. 2012).

Other studies are more assertive. A 2010 meta-review of the evidence for the health benefits of urban green space concluded that several existing reviews support the assessment that green space offers opportunities for exercise (Lee and Maheswaran 2010). Similarly, another 2010 study concluded landscapes do indeed appear to contribute to the promotion of physical well-being by providing space that encourages higher levels of physical activity (Abraham, Sommerhalder, and Abel 2010).

Such claims are further supported by an analysis of survey data in Bristol, which found respondents who lived closest to a park more likely to achieve recommended levels of physical activity and less likely to be overweight or obese (Coombs et al. 2010). Similarly, a 2005 study based on a secondary analysis of a number of surveys estimated the likelihood of being physically active is more than three times as high for respondents living in residential environments with high levels of greenery, and the likelihood of being overweight or obese about 40 percent less. While conceding limitations to the analysis, the authors suggested that more attention should be paid to environmental facilitators and barriers in order to promote physical activity and weight reduction (Ellaway, Macintyre, and Bonnefoy 2005).

Improved Mental Health

The aesthetic experience of looking at or being in green space can have a positive psychosomatic effect on people by reducing stress, lowering blood pressure, and alleviating cognitive and attention deficit disorders. The potential to relax and to exercise in outdoor green areas can contribute to improved mental health and well-being.

Several recent literature reviews have concluded that green space has the potential to benefit people's mental health and well-being. R. Kaplan and S. Kaplan, influential researchers in this field, developed a theory of how natural environments may have a "restorative effect" and ascribed a combination of attributes to green space, including "aesthetically pleasing stimuli, which promote 'soft fascination'" (Kaplan 1985, Kaplan 1995, and Kaplan and Kaplan 1989, cited in Forest Research 2010).

In its 2010 review, Forest Research concluded there is a strong body of evidence that suggests physical activity in green space has stronger mental health benefits than physical activity in non-green space, and that "more passive forms of usage" can also have a beneficial impact on mental well-being and cognitive function. In some studies this is even related simply to the ability to view green space from afar. A 2010 scoping study similarly concluded that by helping to reduce stress, evoke positive emotions, and restore attention, landscapes have the potential to promote mental well-being (Abraham, Sommerhalder, and Abel 2010). This is also supported by a 2007 literature review citing experimental studies that looked at the effects of green space on attention fatigue, psycho-physiological stress, blood pressure, mental fatigue, and attention deficit (Tzoulas et al. 2007).

Studies analyzing links between the environment and mental health and well-being are frequently based on self-reporting by respondents and have been shown to correlate closely to actual health. For example, a Swedish study in 2003 found statistically significant relationships between the use of urban green space and self-reported levels of stress, regardless of respondents' age, sex, or socioeconomic status (Grahn and Stigsdotter 2003). Dutch researchers in 2010 established that the "restorative quality" of nature is corroborated by surveys in several countries, which show that people consider contact with nature as "one of the most powerful ways to obtain relief from stress" (Van den Berg et al. 2010).

Two UK studies, each taking a very different approach, also support this conclusion. The first is a 2002 study by researchers at the University of Sheffield based on a number of focus groups with users and non-users of urban green space across the UK. The researchers found participants across all focus groups pointed out "psychological reasons" for visiting urban green space. In particular, participants highlighted their use of green space to escape from the city, pollution, and people (Dunnett et al. 2002).

The second is a long-term study based on an analysis of data from responses to the annual British Household Panel Survey from 1991 to 2008. This allowed researchers to trace self-reported psychological health from over 10,000 participants across an 18-year period. The researchers found respondents to be happier when living in urban areas with large amounts of green space

and showing significantly lower mental distress levels and higher well-being (life satisfaction) levels. Importantly, the longitudinal approach made it possible for the researchers to control for other impacts on respondents' lives, such as income, employment status, marital status, health, and housing type (White et al. 2013).

Social Role and Benefits

Successful green space is devised to facilitate diverse activity, and green space that is planned and designed to suit the demographic, cultural, and behavioral characteristics of a local community is more likely to be well used. As such, green space can play an important role in the day-to-day life of children and adults of all ages.

Various vulnerable groups have a high need for access to quality green space. These may include older people, particularly those on low incomes, who need opportunities for physical activity and social contact; people from culturally and linguistically diverse backgrounds with the need for greater social interaction; children and people with decreased mobility that require convenient access closer to home; and people who may have limited territorial range due to financial or religious constraints. In addition, green space can play a significant role for dog owners who have restricted space to exercise their pets at home. Nearby pocket parks, particularly, can play an important role in meeting the needs of these groups as they offer a place for close and affordable leisure and socializing with or in the presence of others. Social benefits of green space include:

Enhanced Cognitive and Motor Skills and Socialization

Green space offers children an area for less restricted and more versatile and challenging play in a social environment. In doing so, children's use of green space can help to improve their creativity, cognitive and motor skills, emotional resilience, and socialization.

Two studies frequently cited with regard to the impact urban green space can have on child development researched the play behavior of children in inner-city Chicago. Both studies found that children playing in green space displayed higher levels of creative play, and played for longer and more collaboratively than children playing in built-up space (USDA Forest Service 2001, cited in Land Use Consultants 2004; Shah and Peck 2005 and Taylor et al. 1998, cited in Forest Research 2010).

These findings are supported by a 2000 Norwegian study, which found that woodland provided a more stimulating and varied play environment for children, and noticeably improved their motor fitness (Fjørtoft and Sageie 2000).

Such impacts are visible to, and valued by, parents and carers, as shown by the University of Sheffield focus groups. Taking children to green space proved to be one of the most frequently mentioned reasons for adults to visit such areas. Respondents widely held the view that green environments provided important spaces where children could explore and "let off steam," and where they could come into contact with nature as well as meet other children and adults—a valuable aspect of children's social development (Dunnett et al. 2002). This is corroborated by the *Monitor of Engagement with the Natural Environment Survey (2009–2012): Analysis of Data Related to Visits with Children*, which showed 15 percent of the total visits taken by the English adult population to be driven by motivations to "entertain" or "play" with children (TNS Travel and Tourism 2012).

Alongside providing potential for more free and unplanned play, parks also provide important space for beneficial planned activities, such as in an education environment. A 2008 study for the UK's then Department for Children, Schools and Families found that children engaged in "learning outside the classroom" activities, including in parks and other natural environments, achieved higher class test scores, high levels of physical fitness and motor skills, as well as increased confidence, self-esteem, and social competences (Malone 2008).

Greater Social Interaction and Community Cohesion

Urban areas are often associated with promoting anonymity or loneliness. Green space, by being publicly accessible and free, and by providing space for events, can offer a natural meeting point for local populations. This contributes to community cohesion and social integration, and supports an increased sense of belonging to an area as well as closer neighborhood ties.

The role of green space in contributing to the promotion of social interaction and community cohesion is certainly a concept that has found interest in the academic world. However, conflicting research results mean there is a lack of consensus on the strength of the existing evidence.

A 2012 study by the Heritage Lottery Fund concluded there is currently little evidence of how culture and heritage, including green space, can contribute to concepts such as social capital, community cohesion, social inclusion, and civic society, when compared with evidence of the benefits derived by individuals (Maeer, Fawcett, and Killick 2012). Authors conducting a systematic literature review in 2013 for the International Federation of Park and Recreation Administration concluded while there are indications across studies that parks promote social cohesion, the small number and varying quality of studies mean the current evidence is weak (Konijnendijk et al. 2013).

Other literature reviews have come to more positive conclusions. A wide-ranging literature review in 2010 determined that existing research certainly suggests landscapes have the potential to promote social well-being through social integration, engagement, participation, and support (Abraham, Sommerhalder, and Abel 2010). Forest Research, meanwhile, cited two studies that each looked at particular demographic groups and the benefits they gain from access to green space. One, a Chicago-based study, looked specifically at older adults in deprived areas and found clear indications of links between access to green space and social integration (Kweon et al. 1998, cited in Forest Research 2010). The second, a Swiss-based study on opportunities for young people to interact with other young people from different cultural backgrounds, found the city's urban forests and parks to be a particularly conducive place for socializing and interaction (Seeland et al. 2009, cited in Forest Research 2010). Based on such studies, Forest Research concluded that evidence suggests green space can offer opportunities to promote interaction between people who may not normally interact, which helps to develop social ties and community cohesion.

A 2004 study also focused on this particular aspect of stronger community ties and suggested natural features and open spaces in residential areas play an important role both in residents' interaction with each other, and their feelings of attachment towards their local community (Kim and Kaplan 2004, cited in Tzoulas et al. 2007). Similarly, a Belgian study found people's perception of the "greenness" of their neighborhood to be the most important predictor of neighborhood satisfaction (Van Herzele and de Vries 2011).

Such studies are further supported by the findings of a Green Space 2007 survey of 20,000 members of the UK public, which found 83 percent of respondents believed parks and green space provided a focal point for their communities. The University of Sheffield research similarly revealed that many of the focus group participants identified green space as "the hub or the spirit of their community." This benefit may well transcend differences in background, as focus groups with women, people from ethnic minorities, and people with disabilities particularly suggested such spaces are "important for whole families" (Dunnett et al. 2002).

Economic Role and Benefits

Green space can play a role in the economy in many ways as it generates financial benefits for local governments, homeowners, and local businesses. Green space can stimulate higher property values, increase foot traffic for nearby businesses, and attract tourists and their dollars. In addition, it has the potential to contribute to a reduction in health care costs by providing a cleaner environment and a place for physical activity.

Government Cost Savings

There are few studies that focus on establishing the monetary value governments and related bodies might derive from the various benefits of green space. However, those that do exist provide positive indications of the likely indirect economic impacts of green space.

Two such studies concentrated on the financial value of environmental benefits. A 2012 study in China, which looked at the potential stormwater runoff reduction in Beijing's green space, valued the financial effect of this at CN¥8.81 per acre (CN¥21.77 per hectare) of open space and calculated the total economic benefit to be equivalent to three quarters of the maintenance cost of the green space. An earlier study that looked at the potential of urban trees in Chicago to act as pollutant removers estimated the annual value of this benefit in the city at US$9.2 million (Nowak 1994 and McPherson et al. 1997, cited in Jim and Chen 2007).

Natural England followed up a claim in another study that asserted people in the UK are 24 percent more likely to be physically active if they have easy access to green space. It estimated if the whole English population had equally easy access to green space, and consequently all were 24 percent more likely to be physically active, the life-cost averted saving to the NHS would be approximately £2.1 billion per annum (Coombs et al. 2010 and Natural England 2009, cited in Richardson and Parker 2011).

Such estimates highlight the difficulties of providing any conclusive financial calculations for these benefits. Rather than attempting to calculate cost savings, many studies instead highlight the current costs to government in meeting socioeconomic and environmental challenges in areas in which green space has a positive effect; thereby implying the ability of green space to reduce these costs. The Forest Research report, for example, cites research that has estimated the current economic impact of urban flooding in England and Wales to lie at £270 million per year with a possible increase to £1 billion and £10 billion per year in the future if no action is taken (Parliamentary Office of Science and Technology 2007 and Evans et al. 2004).

Both Forest Research and the New Economics Foundation (NEF) cite works that estimate the costs of ill health to government. For example, in 2002, the Department of Culture, Media and Sport (DCMS) Strategy Unit estimated the cost of physical inactivity and obesity—risk factors in chronic conditions such as heart disease—to be £8.2 billion for England alone (Department of Culture, Media and Sport Strategy Unit 2002, cited in Esteban 2012). Other studies have attempted to value the cost of mental illness to government, and while figures vary significantly there is consensus that costs range in the tens of billions of pounds. (Sustainable Development Commission 2008, cited in Forest

Research 2010, estimated care costs at £12 billion and costs to the wider economy at £64 per annum; Sainsbury Center for Mental Health 2002, cited in Esteban 2012, estimated costs at £23.1 billion.)

Increased Property and Land Values

Urban residents are more willing to pay a premium on mortgages and rent in order to live in areas close to green space. This results in local increases of property and land values that are linked directly to their proximity to green space.

Studies considering the links between property value and location are most commonly based on the hedonic pricing method, which suggests the value of a good is based on a combination of its various attributes (Smith 2010). Based on this model, many international studies have found strong indications of a correlation between property value and proximity to urban or semi-urban green space.

GLA Economics assessed London house prices in 2010 and found them to be boosted by the total area of green space within a distance of 0.6 miles (1 kilometer) from the property. Based on a model that included green space, built environment, and other location factors (but not socio-economic attributes), the study estimated that location within 1,968 feet (600 meters) of an urban park added between 1.9 and 2.9 percent to the total house value (Smith 2010).

Research by the Royal Institute of Chartered Surveyors in Aberdeen likewise found that location on the edge of a park had the potential to attract a premium of up to 19 percent on house prices. Larger parks with facilities had a more significant impact (Dunse et al. 2007, cited in Maeer et al. 2012). In 2005 CABE Space, a specialist unit of the Commission for Architecture and the Built Environment (CABE), calculated an uplift of typically around 3 to 5 percent for properties within the presence of a "high quality park" (cited in Maeer et al. 2012).

Similar findings are also reported outside the UK. A report commissioned by CABE cites a Dutch study that concluded having a nearby park could raise house prices by 6 percent and a view of a park by 8 percent (Luttik 2000, cited in Woolley and Rose 2004). A study in Dallas found proximity to public green space to be a major factor for many property owners' decision to move to the area (Peiser and Schwann 1993, cited in Woolley and Rose 2004).

In short, there is general agreement that properties in proximity to green space do command a premium price, but the precise value of this uplift will depend on exactly how close the property is, how large the green space is, and what facilities are provided.

Tourism Promotion

Green space is not only appealing to a local population, but also to national and international tourists. Some urban parks—in particular large, well-known parks, such as Regent's Park or Hyde Park in London, Park Güell in Barcelona, or Jardin du Luxembourg in Paris—even contribute to motivating tourists to visit a city. As green space has the capacity to make an urban landscape more attractive, civic officials and marketers will use it to positively promote a city.

Academic literature in recent years has somewhat neglected the topic of how urban parks benefit tourism (Forest Research 2010). In addition, many visitor surveys conducted in green space focus largely on visitor origin and spend, without considering the role these places play in contributing to people's decision to visit a city.

The London Visitor Survey, conducted annually from 2006 to 2010 across London, does however provide strong evidence of the role London's green space plays in attracting both UK and overseas tourists to the city. Data collected from 4,587 visitors to London in 2008 showed that 80 percent of overseas tourists, 74 percent of UK staying visitors, 70 percent of UK day visitors, and 77 percent of London residents ranked "parks and gardens" as "important" or "very important" in their decision to visit or take a day trip to London. Indeed, visitors frequently ranked "parks and gardens" as more important than other options such as "theatre/music/arts performances" or "shopping/markets." (The authors indicate the surveys were conducted during the day, perhaps skewing the research by omitting evening visitors.) Satisfaction rates were also generally high, with an average of 3.92 across all groups, with five equaling "excellent" (TNS Travel and Tourism 2008).

Business Location

In addition to attracting leisure visitors to a city, green space is a factor for decision-makers choosing to locate their business in a certain area. This is driven by the draw of green space for workers, as well as for residents and visitors, as it can positively influence an area's desirability, which can increase customer footfall.

Some publications identify a positive correlation between green space and decisions related to business location, particularly for small consumer-facing businesses (see publications such as Woolley and Rose 2004 for CABE Space, or Shah and Peck 2005 for NEF). NEF cites 1999 research by US-based The Trust for Public Land, which concluded small businesses rate non-built up green space as the highest priority when choosing their location (The Trust for Public Land 1999, cited in Shah and Peck 2005).

Overall, however, there is little evidence of the effect of green space on the decision to locate a business in a certain area. Forest Research concluded there is very little strong or reliable evidence of the impact of green space on economic growth and investments. In a 2009 report The Trust for Public Land looked at seven measurable attributes of city park systems that provide economic value and did not include business location as a factor (Harnik and Welle 2009).

Likewise, and perhaps tellingly, existing city monitors such as Mercer's *Quality of Living Worldwide City Ranking* and Cushman & Wakefield's *European Cities Monitor* which rank cities in order to inform salary levels or aid location decision-making for businesses, do not explicitly include green space as indicators (Mercer 2012; Cushman & Wakefield 2011).

Another strong suggestion of the apparent limited importance business decision-makers place on proximity to green space is provided by City of London Corporation's own polls among businesses—both consumer-focused and non-consumer focused—and the employees in the Square Mile. Survey results from 2009 show only 4 percent of businesses and 3 percent of city executives agreed "more parks, open space, gardens" are a way to improve the area as a place to do business, and only 13 percent of workers identified "more parks, open space, gardens" as a priority to improve the area as a place to work.

These findings stand in stark contrast to the 2007 Green Space survey, which revealed that 82 percent of people believe high quality green parks and spaces encourage people and businesses to locate in a certain area. While surprising at first glance, the results may suggest a differentiation needs to be drawn between the benefits people attribute to having green space close to where employees live, as opposed to where they work.

Chapter 1
Green Space and Stormwater Management Practice

Stormwater management should be applied to the planning of all green space as it plays a very important role in the maintenance of urban ecological systems. Indeed, a stormwater system, when properly designed, should function like "a sponge of city" both absorbing and conserving water. Runoff can cause significant problems for landowners, local governments, and municipal water departments. Sediment can fill drainage ditches and channels triggering flooding, as well as filling rivers, lakes, and estuaries, which can devastate wildlife habitats, degrade water quality, and require extensive restoration. As high stream velocity causes bank erosion and pushes sedimentation downstream it has the potential to destroy valuable habitats and property.

Flooding and its associated problems impact large urban populations around the world. New soil must be brought in to counter erosion and replace soil that has been washed away. The buildup of sediment must be removed from culverts, storm sewers, and navigable waters to restore their functional capacity. In addition, runoff carries nutrients, heavy metals, oils, greases, pathogens, and other materials that accumulate on the land between rains causing damage to property and waterways.

Proper planning can prevent or diminish stormwater problems and is easier and less expensive than, for example, restoring water infrastructure or rebuilding flooded properties. Creative and imaginative design can produce functional stormwater systems that also offer aesthetic amenities and recreational opportunities as well as minimizing maintenance, supporting wildlife habitats, and providing irrigation and fire protection. All too often inadequate or improper design and construction has produced unsightly and unsafe facilities that do not perform well and which quickly become maintenance problems. Public acceptance of such projects is understandably poor and the entire concept suffers as a result.

The following guide to stormwater management principles and best practices has been adapted from *Stormwater Management: A Guide for Floridians* prepared by Eric H. Livingston and Ellen McCarron for the Florida Department of Environmental Regulation. It is intended as a source of general information for design professionals interested in the planning and design of these systems. Sound planning and well-considered design can contribute to sustainable systems that are aesthetically pleasing, safe, efficient, adaptable, and beneficial to the community.

General Principles of Stormwater Management

These 14 general principles will contribute to the optimum design of a stormwater management system:

1. It is considerably more efficient and cost-effective to prevent problems than to correct them later. Sound land-use planning is the essential first step.

2. Every piece of land is part of a larger watershed. A stormwater management system for each development project should be based on, and supported by, a plan for the entire space.

3. A stormwater management system should mimic and use the features and functions of natural stormwater systems, which are largely capital, energy, and maintenance cost free. Design should seek to improve the effectiveness of natural systems, rather than to negate, replace, or ignore them.

4. The volume, rate, timing, and pollutant load of stormwater after development of a management system should closely approximate the conditions that occurred before development. To the greatest extent possible, the perviousness of the site should be maintained, and the rate of runoff should be slowed.

5. A stormwater management system should maximize on-site storage of stormwater. Provision for storage can reduce peak runoff rates; aid in groundwater recharge; provide settling of pollutants; lower the probability of downstream flooding, stream erosion, and sedimentation; and provide water for other beneficial uses.

6. Stormwater runoff should never be discharged directly to surface or ground water. It should be routed over a longer distance, through grassed swales, wetlands, vegetated buffers, and other areas designed to increase overland flow.

7. A stormwater management system, especially one that emphasizes the use of vegetation, should be planned, constructed, and stabilized in advance of the facilities that will discharge into it; i.e. at the start of site disturbance and construction.

8. The design of a stormwater management system must begin with the outlet or point of outflow from the project. The downstream conveyance system should be evaluated to ensure it has the capacity to accept the discharge without adverse downstream effects.

9. Wherever possible, the components of a stormwater management system should be constructed on natural topographic contours. This will minimize erosion and stabilization problems caused by excessive water velocity, and slow the runoff, allowing for greater infiltration and filtering.

10. Stormwater is a component of total water resources and should not be discarded casually. Rather it should be used to replenish water resources and may be used for irrigation (farms, lawns, parks, and golf courses), recreational lakes, groundwater recharge, industrial cooling and process water, and other non-potable domestic uses.

11. Practical, multiple-use temporary storage basins should be an integral component of a stormwater management system. Recreational areas (sports fields, tennis courts, and volleyball courts), neighborhood parks, and even parking facilities provide excellent settings for temporary storage of stormwater.

12. Storage areas should be designed with curving shorelines. This increases the length of the shore and can create space for the growth of littoral vegetation that can provide pollutant filtering and a more diversified aquatic habitat.

13. Vegetated buffer strips should be retained in their natural state and created along the banks of all bodies of water. They prevent erosion, trap sediment, filter runoff, provide public access, enhance site amenities, and function as a floodplain during periods of high water.

14. A stormwater management system must be maintained and looked after. The key to effective maintenance is the clear assignment of responsibilities and regular inspections to determine maintenance needs. Designers should make their systems as simple, natural, and maintenance-free as possible.

Stormwater Best Management Practices

Stormwater Best Management Practices (BMPs) refer to the methods used to achieve satisfactory water quality and quantity at a minimum cost for a given set of circumstances. Source controls are considered central to the application of stormwater BMPs; they are used to manage the volume, rate, and quality of runoff, and a coordinated system of source controls can minimize adverse effects of stormwater by preventing and reducing excess flow and nonpoint source pollution—pollution from many diffuse sources—before it reaches a water collection system.

The design of a stormwater management system is not—or should not be—an afterthought. Rather, it must be an integral part of site planning for every project in order to achieve the desired objectives of flood and water quality protection, erosion control, and improved aesthetics and recreation.

Each project will present different conditions and therefore necessitate different requirements. Indeed, as each site has natural and unnatural attributes that influence the type and configuration of a stormwater management system, the many variations in climate, soil, topography, geology, and planned land use require site-specific design. For example, infiltration practices, such as integrated retention areas in open or landscaped green space, are recommended for sandy soils, while detention and wetland treatment is advocated in natural low areas and isolated wetlands. Figures 1.1 and 1.2 summarize a number of BMP types according to their feasibility for different soil types and watershed sizes.

Stormwater BMPs can be classified into two broad categories—Non-structural and Structural. Non-structural controls are prevention oriented and very cost-effective, and are intended to improve stormwater quality by reducing the generation and accumulation of potential runoff pollutants at or near their sources. They are the first line of defense and include practices such as land use planning and management, wetlands and floodplain protection, public education, fertilizer and pesticide application control, solid waste collection and disposal, street cleaning, and "good housekeeping" techniques on construction sites. Structural controls are used to regulate stormwater volume

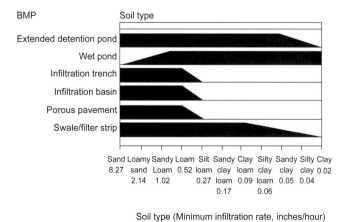

Figure 1.1. BMPs for different soil types

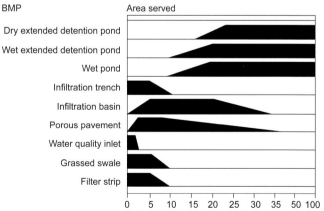

Figure 1.2. BMPs for different watershed sizes

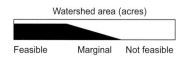

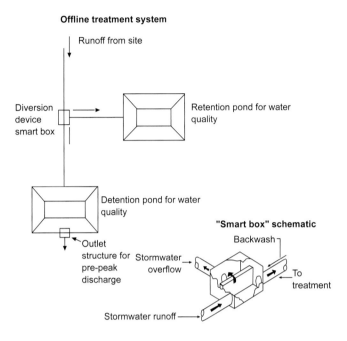

Offline treatment system

Runoff from site

Diversion device smart box

Retention pond for water quality

Detention pond for water quality

Outlet structure for pre-peak discharge

"Smart box" schematic

Backwash

Stormwater overflow

To treatment

Stormwater runoff

Figure 1.3. Schematic of dual-pond offline treatment system

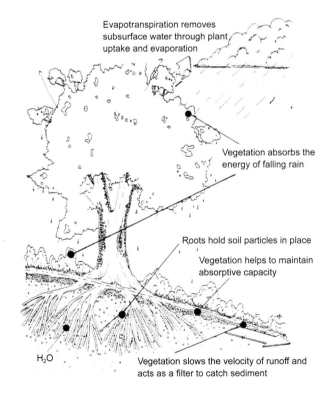

Evapotranspiration removes subsurface water through plant uptake and evaporation

Vegetation absorbs the energy of falling rain

Roots hold soil particles in place

Vegetation helps to maintain absorptive capacity

H₂O

Vegetation slows the velocity of runoff and acts as a filter to catch sediment

Figure 1.4. Erosion control by vegetation cover

and peak discharge rate. They are also employed to reduce the magnitude of pollutants in discharge water through physical containment or flow restrictions that facilitate settling, filtration, percolation, chemical treatment, or biological uptake. These practices are typically land intensive, require proper long-term maintenance, and can be costly, especially in already urbanized areas.

It is common to take a multi-BMP approach to managing the quantity and quality of stormwater runoff. This is referred to as a "BMP treatment train" in which various controls are laid out in series in order to perform multiple actions to best effect. The following source control measures are intended to serve as basic models, and it is important to note that although the different BMPs are discussed individually, they often work together as part of a total system.

Online Versus Offline BMPs

Online BMPs capture all of the runoff from a drainage area and temporarily store it before discharging it to surface waters. They primarily provide flood control benefits, while water quality benefits are secondary. Offline BMPs divert the first flush—the initial surface runoff of a rainstorm—for treatment and isolate it from the remaining stormwater, which is managed for flood control. Offline retention is the most effective water quality protection BMP because the diverted first flush is not discharged to surface waters. Rather, it is stored to be gradually removed through infiltration, evaporation, and evapotranspiration.

Figure 1.3 is a schematic of a dual-pond offline treatment system in which a diversion device, or "smart box," directs the first flush of stormwater into the retention pond. Once filled, it routes the remaining runoff into the detention pond for flood control.

The Importance of Vegetation

Vegetation provides several benefits for managing stormwater, and particularly for erosion control as Figure 1.4 illustrates. Vegetation absorbs the energy of falling rain and removes subsurface water through infiltration; roots hold soil particles in place maintaining their capacity to absorb water; and runoff velocity is slowed, reducing peak discharge rate.

Vegetation is especially important in reducing erosion and sedimentation during construction of a stormwater system. In fact, sedimentation at construction sites can be reduced by up to 90 percent by phasing and limiting the removal of vegetation, by decreasing the area that is cleared, and limiting the time bare land is exposed to rainfall. Large areas of cleared land should be mulched and seeded to provide immediate temporary cover if construction is not to occur within seven days. In addition, special consideration should be given to the maintenance of vegetative cover on areas highly prone to erosion, such as erodible soils, steep or long slopes, stormwater conveyances, and stream banks.

Stormwater BMPs that use vegetative cover include overland sheet flow, grassed swales and channels, infiltration areas, and grassed discharge or flow areas for roof drainage. All are particularly suited to residential, transportation, and recreational developments, and also can be used in commercial and industrial sites.

The amount and nature of topsoil and vegetation are important factors affecting the infiltration of stormwater. A thick layer of topsoil with dense sod provides excellent natural infiltration and areas under development that are to be revegetated should be covered by an adequate layer of topsoil. The original topsoil at the side should be removed and stockpiled for reuse to provide a minimum of 4 inches (10.2 centimeters) over areas that have a porous sub-soil. In areas of heavy clay, 6 to 8 inches (15.2 to 20.3 centimeters) of topsoil will provide proper plant growth and create absorbent soil.

Infiltration (Retention) Practices

Infiltration is a natural part of the hydrologic cycle in undeveloped areas, and precipitation can be absorbed into the ground, replenishing the groundwater and feeding trees and other plants. Infiltration practices similarly retain stormwater onsite, allowing it to infiltrate into the ground or to evaporate. These practices reduce the volume of stormwater and are the most effective for lessening pollution since the first flush is typically not discharged to surface waters. By limiting the volume of stormwater, retention practices help to reduce its effects on estuaries, which are vulnerable to too much fresh water.

The amount of retention and infiltration depends primarily on the soil. Successful use of retention practices requires appropriate site conditions to ensure stormwater will infiltrate within 24 to 72 hours. Coarse-grained sandy soils have excellent infiltration capacity, however this diminishes as soils begin to contain higher amounts of fine-grained clays and silts. To protect groundwater from contamination, the seasonal high water table and bedrock should be at least 3 feet (90 centimeters) beneath the bottom of the retention practice. Special precautions must be taken to protect the groundwater in areas where limestone is near the surface and sinkholes are common.

In areas with appropriate site conditions, offline infiltration practices should be used wherever possible, including retention basins and infiltration areas, grassed swales, and infiltration trenches. Offline infiltration can be easily incorporated into landscaped and open green space such as natural or excavated grassed depressions, recreational areas, and even landscaped parking area islands. Some infiltration practices can be designed as landscaped rock gardens or picturesque creek beds, and lawns, especially on waterfront property, can be designed to temporarily store runoff. Since retention areas are frequently designed to remain dry when not in use, they can often provide multiple purposes, for example, stormwater management during wet weather and recreational spaces or parking facilities during dry weather.

Effective design and proper installation can help ensure infiltration practices meet the challenges of safety, maintenance, efficiency, and aesthetics. However, as with any construction project, effective solutions must be carefully planned and developed and considered as part of the entire system.

Dry Retention Basins or Areas

Nearly every land use in a developing area can effectively and economically incorporate on-site offline retention into its design. If site conditions will not allow total infiltration of the first flush, then at least part of the first flush can be infiltrated for pretreatment before the stormwater enters a wet detention or wetland system for final treatment.

On a small scale, lawns, parking islands, and small landscaped areas can all be used as retention basins to store stormwater and allow it to infiltrate. Such areas are especially appropriate as elements of a BMP treatment train where raised storm sewer inlets are placed in the retention area allowing some treatment before excess stormwater is routed to a detention facility.

On a larger scale, retention areas can be designed into open spaces of an entire development or park system. Proper design of these retention systems can contribute to successful, useful, and attractive results, and large retention areas can serve as parks or community recreation areas during dry periods.

The side slopes of infiltration areas should be gentle enough to mow and properly shaped to blend with the surrounding topography. When intended for recreational use, grassy side slopes or banks can provide an amphitheater for spectator seating, and also serve to contain balls in the playing area, avoiding the need for a fence.

Good vegetative cover and proper drying are extremely important in the design and development of multiple-use retention and recreation facilities. The ground must be properly graded to a 2 percent slope (more on poorly drained soils) to provide adequate surface drainage, and it must facilitate appropriate recreational use and avoid low spots that might remain wet. In some situations, underdrains may be needed to stimulate infiltration and help eliminate standing water. Reducing the possibility of standing water can avoid problems of weeds, algae, and mosquitoes, and the multiple uses of the stormwater system can be realized.

The natural characteristics of the site must be respected and used properly. Naturalistic retention areas in green space can be created in naturalized or wooded areas, reducing maintenance. Indeed, with sensitive placement, imaginative design, careful construction, and appropriate landscaping, stormwater retention facilities can effectively protect property and water quality and still be an aesthetically pleasing part of the community environment.

Grassed Swales

A swale, or grassed waterway, is:

· a shallow trench that has side slopes less than 3 feet (90 centimeters) horizontal and 1 foot (30 centimeters) vertical;

· designed to contain standing or flowing water only after a rainfall;

· planted with or has vegetation suitable for soil stabilization, stormwater treatment, and nutrient uptake;

· designed to take soil erodability, soil percolation, slope, slope length, and drainage area into account so as to prevent erosion and reduce stormwater pollutant load.

Swales are considered an on-line practice, traditionally used primarily for stormwater conveyance. As with other retention practices, the effectiveness of pollutant removal depends on the volume of stormwater that can be infiltrated through vegetation and into the soil.

Used alone, swales must percolate 80 percent of runoff from a 3-inch (7.6-centimeter) rainfall within 72 hours to provide proper water quality benefits. However, this is often impossible because of soil or slope and the greatest utility of a swale is as a pretreatment conveyance system to reduce pollutants before stormwater enters a retention and/or detention basin, or wetland. Thus, swales should be seen as an important component of a BMP treatment train.

The effectiveness of pollutant removal and the infiltration capability of a swale can be improved by placing small check dams along its length, or using raised culverts to cause stormwater to pond. This effectively slows and retains runoff to allow some to soak into the ground and be filtered by vegetation. Figure 1.5 is an example of a swale with a cross block.

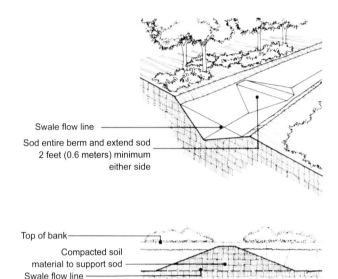

Swale flow line

Sod entire berm and extend sod 2 feet (0.6 meters) minimum either side

Top of bank

Compacted soil material to support sod

Swale flow line

Figure 1.5. Swale with cross block

The feasibility of swales depends on land use and site characteristics. The linear structure of swales means they are frequently used in the treatment of runoff from roads and streets, along property boundaries, and in and around parking lots.

Public education is essential for the maintenance of swales. Green space users should be informed about the function and care of swales; for example, leaves and branches can cause blockages, and the pollutants of debris or oil, should they be disposed of in a swale, can be delivered to downstream waters in which case a benefit of the swale would be lost.

Infiltration Trenches

Land costs can be so prohibitive in many urban areas that retention basins are not feasible. In such cases an offline infiltration trench can serve as the primary component of a treatment train. As Figure 1.6 illustrates, infiltration trenches consist of a long, narrow excavation ranging from 3 feet to 12 feet (90 centimeters to 3.7 meters) in depth, depending on stormwater volume, soil, and water table conditions. It is backfilled with stone aggregate, allowing for the first flush of stormwater to be temporarily stored in the voids between aggregate materials. Stored runoff then infiltrates into the surrounding soil.

Trench bottoms should be at least 4 feet (1.2 meters) above the seasonal high water table to prevent groundwater contamination.

Another important consideration for infiltration trenches is use of the treatment train concept to maximize water quality benefits, reduce maintenance requirements, and prevent the physical clogging of these systems by sediment, leaves, and other materials. Limestone aggregate should not be used since it has the tendency to cement together, thus reducing the voids in which the stormwater is stored.

Infiltration trenches can be located on the surface or below the ground. Surface trenches receive sheet flow runoff directly from adjacent areas after a grass buffer has filtered it. They are typically used in residential areas where smaller loads of sediment and oil can be trapped by grassed filter strips that are at least 20 feet (6.1 meters) wide. While surface trenches may be more susceptible to sediment accumulations, their accessibility makes them easier to maintain. Surface trenches can be used in parking areas and in narrow landscaped areas.

Underground trenches can accept runoff from storm sewers, and while they can be incorporated in many development situations, discretion must be exercised with their applicability. Inlets to underground trenches must include trash racks, catch basins, and baffles to reduce sediment, leaves, debris, and oils and greases. The most commonly used underground trench is an exfiltration system in which runoff is diverted into an oversized perforated pipe placed within an aggregate envelope. The first flush of stormwater is stored in the pipe and exfiltrates out of the holes through the gravel and into the surrounding soil.

Pretreatment is essential to prevent clogging and the maintenance or replacement of underground trenches can be very difficult and expensive, especially if they are placed beneath parking areas or pavement. Routine maintenance consists of vacuuming debris from the catch basin inlets and, if needed, using high pressure hoses to wash clogging materials out of the pipe.

Parking Areas

Paved parking areas are one of the largest generators of runoff and polluted stormwater. Figure 1.7 illustrates one effective design of a parking area, which incorporates multiple BMPs. Recessed landscape islands function as small retention and pretreatment areas and curb cuts allow stormwater to more easily flow into these islands. Raised storm sewer inlets help filter heavy metals, oils, and greases, and provide retention and infiltration of the first flush before stormwater is routed to a detention system.

Porous concrete is a cost-effective and viable BMP with widespread applicability for parking areas because it allows water to percolate into the underlying soil. Parking areas paved with porous concrete can remain pervious and act as a large retention area, thereby reducing stormwater volume, peak discharge rate,

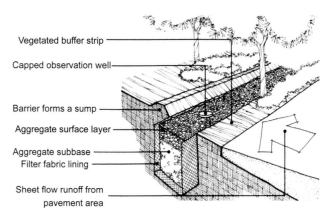

Figure 1.6. Infiltration channels

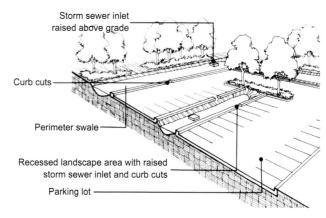

Figure 1.7. BMPs for parking areas

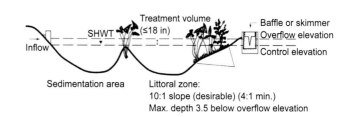

Figure 1.8. Typical wet detention components

and pollutant load. In addition, it eliminates water pockets and provides a safer, skid-resistant surface. However, it is only feasible and cost effective on sites with gentle slopes, permeable soils, and relatively deep water table and bedrock levels.

When properly designed, installed, and maintained, porous concrete has load-bearing strength and longevity similar to that of conventional concrete. Only professional teams of engineers and contractors familiar with the properties of porous concrete should undertake its design and installation, and during construction it is essential that effective erosion and sediment control practices be used to prevent clogging. Regular inspection and maintenance is necessary for preserving its high infiltration rate and the surface should be routinely checked for debris, ponding, clogging, or other damage after prolonged storms. Regular vacuum sweeping should be performed to prevent clogging and high pressure steam cleaning may be needed annually.

Detention Practices

Detention systems are storage areas that maintain a permanent level of water even after stormwater discharge has ceased. These permanent lakes and ponds, if properly planned and constructed, afford multiple benefits, including the potential for 'lake-front' property, possibilities for recreation and wildlife habitats, water for irrigation and fire protection, and even a source of fill. Detention practices also provide flood protection and very good removal of stormwater pollutants.

Permanently wet detention systems and wetland treatment systems are likely to be preferred BMPs in locations that have slowly percolating soils, high water tables, and flat terrain. The stormwater BMP treatment train is especially applicable to detention systems and the use of swales, landscape infiltration areas, and perimeter swale/berms for pretreatment will greatly improve the pollutant removal effectiveness, aesthetics, and longevity of a detention system.

Figure 1.8 illustrates the basic components of a wet detention system used for flood control and water quality enhancement. Essentially, a wet detention lake consists of a permanent water pool, an overlying zone in which the design runoff volume temporarily increases the depth while it is stored and released at the allowed peak discharge rate, and a shallow littoral zone in which wetland plants biologically remove dissolved stormwater pollutants such as metals and nutrients. During a storm, runoff replaces the treated water detained within the permanent pool after a previous storm. Wet detention lakes are often used in series, with swale interconnections.

The technical design criteria for detention systems, established by the Florida Department of Environmental Regulation and Florida's Water Management Districts, is for readers' reference only and addresses general concerns that are important to safe and efficient operation of such systems. This includes evaluation of runoff hydrographs for storms of various size and frequency; determination of level of flood protection and rate of stormwater release; design requirements to maximize pollutant removal; provisions for maintenance; and provisions for emergency overflow to protect adjacent and downstream properties.

Once the technical requirements have been established, they must be translated into physical reality through competent design and construction. The same set of technical requirements can be met through a traditional engineering solution or through creative design with full appreciation for aesthetics, maintenance, safety, and multiple-use considerations.

Regional detention systems can be established to provide stormwater management for several projects within a watershed. In addition, regional facilities can provide for water quality enhancement and flood protection for existing runoff problems and, if located and designed as part of an overall stormwater master plan, they can address stormwater management needs associated with future development. Regional facilities also offer many advantages such as economy of scale for construction and operation costs and greater overall effectiveness, and regional detention systems can provide recreational and open space benefits in the urban environment.

Maintenance of Stormwater Systems

The ultimate success of any stormwater program depends on proper maintenance. If a system is not properly cared for, the possibility of failure and subsequent downstream damage is very real. Sooner or later, damage will require investment in management facilities, which could have been prevented.

Continuing maintenance should be incorporated into the planning and design of a stormwater system. Soil conditions, topography, watershed size, land use, slope of vegetated banks, and overall effectiveness will all have a bearing, as does the consideration of who is ultimately responsible for maintenance and safety. Proper handling of these elements during design and construction can minimize upkeep activities and costs.

Stormwater systems are part of the public infrastructure and should be maintained physically and financially by the government in the same way. Proper easements and adequate access to all facilities, as well as the financing of required maintenance, must be a necessary part of any stormwater management program. Indeed, counteracting the potential for major downstream damage and degraded water quality from uncontrolled runoff is essential to the health of the community.

Chapter 2
Design Guidelines for Green Space in the Community

The following guidelines have been adapted from the County of Los Angeles' *Park Design Guidelines and Standards*, which are intended to facilitate the Los Angeles County Department of Parks and Recreation in achieving high quality design and environmental stewardship in all aspects of parkland development. They are provided here for reference only and readers can obtain more relevant and regional information on green space design from their local council bodies. Design professionals are also responsible for complying with all regulatory and permit requirements associated with a project.

Spatial Organization

Spatial organization is an important element of green space design and care and consideration needs to be given to the use of each space, the relationship between activities, and future expansion opportunities.

Green space is often programmed for multiple functions and should be designed to allow for flexibility of use. Thoughtful spatial organization encourages social interaction and user participation, which allows many diverse activities to occur simultaneously, while facilitating administrative visibility and control of the site. For areas used by different age groups, consideration of user compatibility must be evaluated when determining the adjacency of site features. Construction cost, mechanical systems layout, user safety, site amenities, and provisions for universal accessibility will also affect these variables.

The following spatial organizational principles are expressed as typical criteria in order to describe how individual spaces can complement one another to form functional areas, and how functional areas support one another to form cohesive site design.

Physical Access and Adjacency Compatibility

Giving consideration to physical access and the compatibility of adjacent areas can assist in meeting requirements related to safety, privacy, concentration of activities, ease of operations, and administration.

· Strategically place active and passive spaces to allow diverse activities and diverse user groups participating in both planned activities and free play to occur simultaneously, as Figure 2.1 illustrates.

· Group activities to maximize desirable effects, such as accessibility, control of participants, or multiple uses; and separate activities to minimize conflicts, including noise and degree of physical activity.

· Consider neighbors and surrounding communities when locating green space features that may be potential sources of disturbance, such as sports facilities, field lights, group amenities, swimming pools, and gymnasiums.

· Locate restroom buildings within a 150-foot (45-meter) radius of recreation fields and a 100-foot (30-meter) radius of children's play areas.

· Locate trash enclosures at least 50 feet (15 meters) from all buildings.

· Locate maintenance yards away from children's play areas.

· Screen maintenance yards from adjacent activities.

· Arrange activity areas to encourage casual interaction among users, offer transitional areas for lounging, and provide visual access from one area to another.

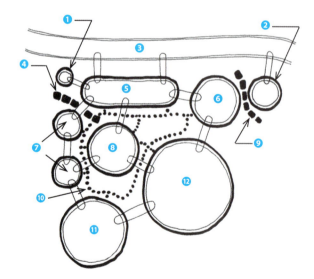

① Trash enclosure
② Maintenance yard
③ Street
④ Barrier
⑤ Parking area
⑥ Sports court
⑦ Children's play areas
⑧ Gym/restroom/office
⑨ Buffer
⑩ Pedestrian circulation
⑪ Passive play and picnic areas
⑫ Active recreation fields

Figure 2.1. Park adjacency compatibility diagram

· Locate facilities that draw large numbers of users, such as gymnasiums, recreational centers, and pool facilities, near or within view of established public transit routes to encourage and facilitate alternative modes of travel.

· Locate parking areas near major site features to facilitate users carrying equipment and/or supplies to their destination.

Visual Access

· Visual access from one area to another is an important consideration for administrative control, as well as for green space users' awareness of adjacent activities.

Acoustics

· Care should be taken in the placement of green space features that facilitate activities generating potentially disruptive noise.

· Locate and buffer spaces to minimize the impact of park activities on adjacent land users. Figure 2.2 suggests the placement of a "quiet zone" between a park site and residential area in order to buffer noise.

Security and Safety

Planners and designers should understand and utilize strategies of crime prevention through environmental design (CPTED) in order to create a safe and secure green space. The following strategies are recommended by Susan Manheimer, Chief of Police, San Mateo Police Department, San Mateo, California.

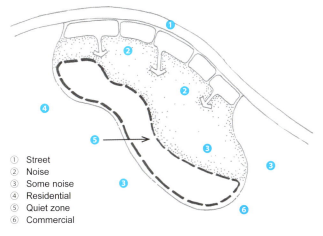

① Street
② Noise
③ Some noise
④ Residential
⑤ Quiet zone
⑥ Commercial

Figure 2.2. Acoustical consideration diagram

Natural Surveillance

Natural surveillance increases potential offenders' threat of apprehension by increasing the perception they can be seen. The strategic placement of physical features and activity areas can maximize users' visibility and foster positive social interaction among legitimate users, making potential offenders feel increased scrutiny and limitations on their escape routes.

· Place building windows overlooking sidewalks and parking areas.

· Locate features and activities near passing vehicular traffic.

· Create landscape designs that offer surveillance, especially in proximity to designated and opportunistic points of entry.

· Use the shortest and least sight-limiting fence appropriate for the situation.

· Use transparent weather vestibules at building entrances.

· Avoid placing lights that create blind spots for potential observers and/or miss critical areas.

· Ensure potential problem areas, such as pathways, stairs, entrances, exits, parking areas, kiosks, bus stops, children's play areas, recreation areas, pools, storage areas, trash enclosures, and recycling areas, are well lit.

· Avoid too-bright security lighting that creates blinding glare and/or deep shadows, hindering the view for potential observers. Install more fixtures if using lower intensity lights.

· Control glare with shielded or cut-off luminaries.

· Light people's faces, including those of potential offenders, by placing lighting along pathways and other pedestrian-use areas at proper heights.

· Enable passive surveillance with openwork or transparent gates and/or along corridors and trails.

Natural Access Control

Natural access control limits the opportunity for crime by differentiating between public space and private space. The strategic placement of entrances, exits, fencing, lighting, and landscaping can limit access or control flow in, out, and/or through a green space.

· Use a single, clearly identifiable point of entry.

· Use structures to divert people to reception areas.

· Plant low, thorny bushes beneath ground level windows.

· Eliminate design features that provide access to roofs or upper levels.

Natural Territorial Reinforcement

Natural territorial reinforcement promotes social control by increasing the definition of a space and its proprietary concern. Creating a sense of stakeholders' common vested interest in a space can discourage crime because of the increased perception the area is guarded. This can make legitimate users feel safe, while making potential offenders aware of the risk of apprehension or scrutiny.

· Display notices of security systems at access points.

· Place amenities, such as seating or vending machines, in common areas to attract larger numbers of desired users.

· Schedule activities in common areas to increase proper usage, attract more people, and increase the perception the area is monitored.

Maintenance

Ensure regular maintenance of property and facilities to indicate greater control of a site and therefore greater intolerance of disorder and crime. The "broken windows theory" is a valuable tool in understanding the importance of maintenance for deterring crime. The theory proposes a zero-tolerance approach to property maintenance by claiming the presence of a broken window will entice vandals to break more windows in the vicinity. Thus, the sooner broken windows are fixed, the less likely such vandalism will occur.

Additional Security Features

· All visual overlooks must have an open and unobstructed view of the green space and a 10-foot-wide (3-meter-wide) pedestrian walk for law enforcement accessibility.

· Decorative window guards, such as ornamental bars, screening, or panels are recommended for enhanced security. Window guards must not impede passive surveillance.

· Security cameras are recommended for all green space sites.

Buildings

Building design strategies can contribute to conservation efforts in a number of ways. Consideration should be given to remodeling instead of replacing existing buildings wherever possible, building on the minimum space necessary to satisfy functional space requirements, and designing multi-functional spaces. In addition, considerable electrical and thermal energy can be saved through building design that incorporates day lighting and other passive energy-conserving strategies appropriate to the local climatic environment.

Contextual Site Considerations

· Locate structures to recognize, preserve, and protect established major vistas.

· Consider the distinctive qualities and character of surrounding vernacular architecture and incorporate those qualities into the design of structures and features where appropriate.

· Ensure structure designs and historical restorations are sensitive to environmental, cultural, and historical context.

· Implement unifying architectural features, such as forms, details, materials, and colors, in structures located throughout the green space.

· Consider site variables, such as size, shape, topography, orientation, views, and natural features, as well as climatic

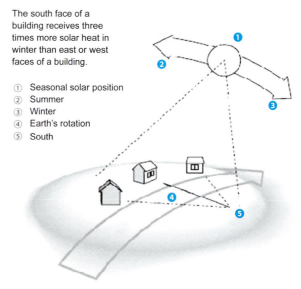

The south face of a building receives three times more solar heat in winter than east or west faces of a building.

① Seasonal solar position
② Summer
③ Winter
④ Earth's rotation
⑤ South

Figure 2.3. Building orientation

24

variables, such as severe or temperate, when locating structures in a green space.

· Consider a building's spatial organization and site orientation when undertaking additions and alterations, which should be planned to support functional and site-sensitive expansion. As illustrated in Figure 2.3, the south face of a building receives three times more solar heat in winter than east or west facing sides. In summer, east and west faces receive the most solar heat.

Sustainability Considerations

· Perform an analysis of all building construction and roof replacement projects to determine the potential benefits of using photovoltaics, or solar panels.

· Perform an analysis of energy and environmental design criteria as they apply to the design and construction of a building project.

· Design new buildings and remodels to meet local sustainability regulations and suggested criteria.

Regulatory Considerations

· Design buildings in accordance with all applicable jurisdictional laws and regulations.

Restroom Buildings

Spatial Considerations

· Locate restroom buildings to ensure they are visible and in close proximity to parking areas and public streets.

· Locate restroom buildings within a 100-foot (30-meter) radius of children's play areas and within a 150-foot (46-meter) radius of active recreation fields.

Amenities

· Provide ample paving around the perimeter of the building for ease of accessibility and entry.

· Coat interior and exterior walls with anti-graffiti finish.

· Incorporate natural ventilation and lighting wherever possible.

· Provide interior electrical overhead lighting with timers.

· Provide vandal-resistant exterior security lighting.

· Provide floor drains in each stall.

· Locate drinking fountains and hand sinks outside restroom buildings; these should cater for people with and without disabilities.

Regulatory Considerations

· Provide at least two stalls in each building—one women's and one men's.

· Comply with building codes and other legal requirements.

See Figure 2.4 for an example of a restroom building layout.

Community Buildings

Community buildings are intended to support indoor organized community events, meetings, and activities.

Spatial Considerations

· Locate buildings reasonably close to parking areas and public streets and ensure they are visible.

· Provide a drop-off/pick-up zone near the main entrance.

· Provide a paved area for special events near the main entrance or multipurpose room.

· Ensure ease of entry and prevent pedestrian destruction of planted areas and water infiltration into buildings by providing ample paving around the perimeter of the building.

· Ensure all paved and unpaved areas around the perimeter of the building have a minimum 2 percent slope away from all exterior walls within the limit of the first 10 feet (3 meters).

Amenities

· Provide multi-functional rooms that can be used for a variety of activities for different age groups throughout the day.

· Provide classrooms to accommodate 20 to 30 people.

· Provide resilient flooring, such as linoleum, vinyl composition tile, or rubber tile floor.

· Provide a kitchen that caters to people with and without disabilities.

· Provide restrooms inside the building for people with and without disabilities.

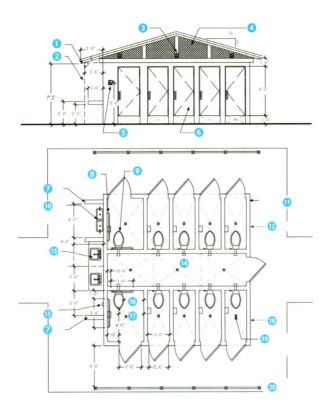

① Roll-up locking doors
② Wing wall
③ Vandal proof outdoor lighting
④ 0.125 in (0.32 cm) woven stainless steel custom vent screen
⑤ Signage for people with and without disabilities
⑥ Metal doors with phenolic finish
⑦ Wing wall
⑧ Stainless steel grab bar for people with disabilities
⑨ Stainless steel toilet for people with and without disabilities
⑩ Drinking fountain for people with and without disabilities
⑪ Split face concrete block
⑫ Women
⑬ Stainless steel sinks with cantilevered counter top
⑭ Mechanical room
⑮ Hand dryer for people with and without disabilities
⑯ 2.7 ft (80 cm) minimum clear
⑰ 3.5 ft (1.1 m) minimum clear
⑱ Men
⑲ 4 in (10cm) satin chrome drain grate
⑳ Semi-transparent screening element raised 1 ft (30 cm) above floor

Figure 2.4. Example of restroom building layout diagram

· Provide bicycle racks, trash receptacles, and drinking fountains near the building entrance. Ensure these cater to people with and without disabilities.

· Provide natural lighting wherever possible.

· Provide security lighting at or nearby the building.

· Provide directional signage from the street to the main entrance.

Regulatory Considerations

· Ensure restrooms comply with building codes and meet all legal requirements.

· Ensure the kitchen meets all local health department requirements.

See Figure 2.5 for an example of a community building layout.

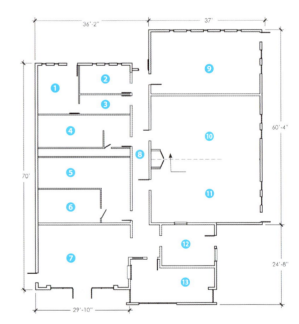

① Mechanical/electrical room, 198 ft² (18.4 m²)
② Storage room 2, 140 ft² (13 m²)
③ Janitor's room 2, 90 ft² (8.4 m²)
④ Men's restroom, 290 ft² (26.9 m²)
⑤ Women's restroom, 375 ft² (34.8 m²)
⑥ Storage room 1, 205 ft² (19 m²)
⑦ Reception room, 587 ft² (54.5 m²)
⑧ Hallway, 333 ft² (30.9 m²)
⑨ Classroom, 664 ft² (61.7 m²)
⑩ Multipurpose room, 1,357 ft² (126.1 m²)
⑪ Partition
⑫ Kitchen, 211 ft² (19.6 m²)
⑬ Office, 282 ft² (26.2 m²)
Total area, 4,788 ft² (444.8 m²)

Figure 2.5. Example of community building layout diagram

Sports Field Concession Stands

Spatial Considerations

· Locate concession stands in close proximity to spectator areas.

· Provide vehicular access to concession stands.

· Locate trash enclosures reasonably close to concession stands.

· Provide ample paving around the perimeter for ease of entry and pedestrian accessibility.

Amenities

· Provide basic kitchen facilities.

· Install resilient flooring, such as linoleum or vinyl composition tile.

· Provide ample in-unit storage space.

· Include a double-door entry for delivery of products and equipment, and a roll-up window for serving.

· Provide natural ventilation and lighting wherever possible.

· Provide security lighting at or near the concession stands.

Regulatory Considerations

· Ensure kitchens comply with building codes and meet all legal requirements.

See Figure 2.6 for an example of a sports field concession stand building layout.

Maintenance Buildings/Yards

Maintenance buildings and yards support a broad spectrum of recreational facilities.

Spatial Considerations

· Provide separate entrances to maintenance yards and parking areas, wherever possible.

· Locate entrance off parking areas if separate entrances to the maintenance yard and parking area is not feasible.

· Provide screening between maintenance yards and green space.

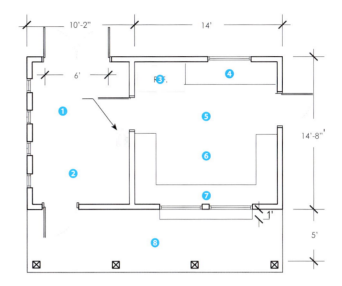

① Hand sink only
② Storage room, 123 ft^2 (11.4 m^2)
③ Referee
④ Counter
⑤ Concession room, 186 ft^2 (17.3 m^2)
⑥ Prepackaged food only
⑦ Counter
⑧ Overhang
Total area, 310 ft^2 (28.8 m^2)

Figure 2.6. Example of sports field concession stand building layout diagram

· Ensure maintenance offices have visible access to adjacent yards.

· Accommodate storage of maintenance vehicles, tools, supplies, and materials in maintenance buildings.

· Provide secured gates and fencing around the perimeter of all maintenance yards.

Amenities

· Provide office space for staff.

· Provide a minimum of one restroom that caters to people with and without disabilities.

· Provide rest/eating areas and kitchenette space.

· Provide roll-up doors for entry.

Regulatory Considerations

· Cover waste items and hazardous materials to mitigate contamination of stormwater runoff.

· Ensure restrooms and kitchenette comply with building codes and meet legal requirements.

See Figure 2.7 for an example of a small maintenance building and yard layout.

Parking Areas

The parking area is a gateway through which many visitors may pass and is often the first and last element of a green space to be viewed. This first impression is very important in establishing the overall feeling and atmosphere conveyed to the user.

Spatial Considerations

· Locate parking areas in close proximity to major activity areas.

· Provide adequate parking spaces to minimize parking on residential and arterial streets.

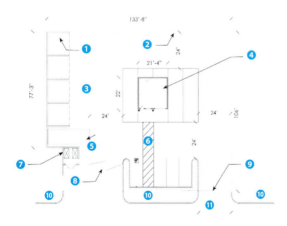

① Four bulk material bins with roof shelter, 15 x 15 ft (4.6 x 4.6 m)
② Tubular steel fence
③ Asphalt paving
④ One bay work area counter with sink and office, 460 ft² (42.7 m²)
⑤ One bulk trash container with cover, 19 x 30 ft (5.8 x 9.1 m)
⑥ Five parking spaces for people with and without disabilities
⑦ Trash enclosure with roof
⑧ Double swing gates
⑨ Tubular steel sliding gate and perimeter fence
⑩ Planted area
⑪ 24 ft (7.3 m) drive isles

Figure 2.7. Example of small maintenance building and yard layout diagram

· Provide parking areas that service and support green space facilities; they should not bisect or segment the site.

· Ensure parking areas are visually unobstructed and highly visible at all times.

· Provide overflow parking for special events.

Amenities

· Provide a barrier gate at vehicular entries, and access barriers at parking area perimeters.

· Provide vegetated screening or visual barriers to prevent vehicle headlights shining into residential areas.

· Provide access for maintenance vehicles.

· Provide wheel stops at all zero curb heights. Ensure wheel stops and curb heights do not impact vehicular clearance.

· Provide ramps for people with disabilities.

· Plant trees at regular intervals to create a canopy to shade vehicles and lower the heat island effect in parking areas.

· Plant trees, shrubs, and ground cover at suitable intervals to break up the continuity of the parking area. Ensure this does not block the view of motorists and pedestrians.

· Provide preferred parking spaces and signage for low-emission and fuel-efficient vehicles at high-use sites.

· Ensure grading and drainage is in line with stormwater BMPs.

Regulatory Considerations

· Provide security lighting that meets current council regulations and local building standards.

· Provide two points of ingress/egress access drives, a turnaround, or a hammerhead for vehicles of all sizes.

· Comply with standards and guidelines for providing access and facilities for people with disabilities.

· Provide parking spaces and clear signage for people with disabilities.

See Figures 2.8—2.13 for examples of parking area curbs and layouts.

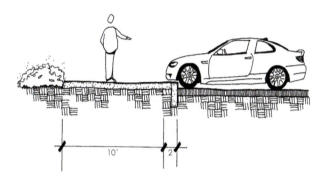

Figure 2.8. Parking area curb—6 in (15.2 cm) curb adjacent primary pedestrian walk

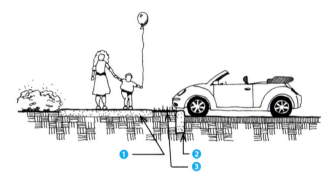

① Walkway width varies
② Concrete curb
③ Low groundcover of turf

Figure 2.9. Parking area curb—6 in (15.2 cm) curb adjacent planted area

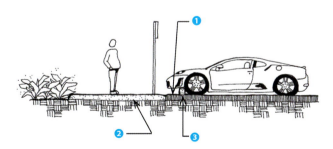

① Allow 2 ft (60 cm) for car overhang
② Walkway width varies
③ Wheel stop

Figure 2.10. Parking area curb—zero curb face at parking stalls for people with disabilities

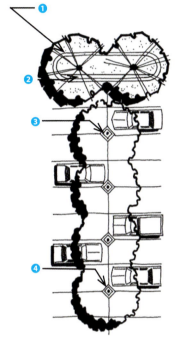

① Curb-height oval planter
② 1 ft (30 cm) step out
③ Minimum of one tree per four parking stalls
④ Curb-height diamond-shaped planters

Figure 2.11. Shade tree layout in parking area

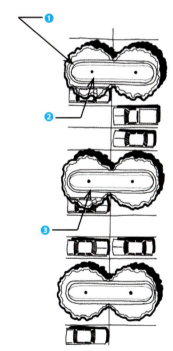

① Curb-height oval planter
② Minimum of one tree per four parking stalls
③ 1 ft (30 cm) step out

Figure 2.12. Shade tree layout in parking area (alternate)

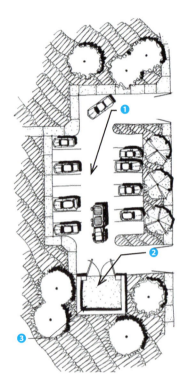

① Bin accessible from parking area
② 12 ft (3.7 m) wide opening
③ Trash enclosure with roof

Figure 2.13. Parking area design with trash bin enclosure

Circulation

Well-connected networks of roads and paths provide an effective means to accommodate all forms of travel including walking, cycling, and public transport. Multiple routes through a well-connected circulation system can help ensure walking and cycling routes are attractive and safe.

· Develop one main entry into the green space to create a sense of arrival.

· Provide one primary path of travel that connects all major use areas, as illustrated in Figure 2.14.

· Provide less-direct secondary paths and non-circulation tertiary paths.

· Locate primary and secondary paths to minimize environmental impacts on the site.

· Frame views to direct attention to landscape features along pathways.

· Provide deliberate focal points such as a circular drop-off or plaza where the network of pedestrian paths, bicycle routes, and vehicular roads meet.

· Locate all fixtures, such as security lights, trash receptacles, drinking fountains, and benches, along pathways.

· Ensure the width of pathways and around amenities caters to people with disabilities.

· Provide access for fire, emergency response, and maintenance vehicles.

Pedestrian

· Provide all pedestrians with open access to the green space and its facilities, and clearly mark accessibility for people with disabilities.

· Separate pedestrian pathways from bicycle routes, vehicular traffic, and entrances where possible.

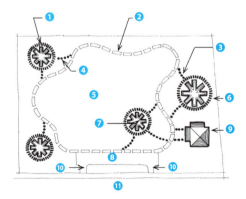

① Activity area with tertiary path, 5 ft (1.5 m) wide
② Primary circulation path, 10 ft (3 m) wide
③ Secondary walkway access path
④ Secondary walkway access path, 6 ft (1.8 m) wide
⑤ Active recreation area
⑥ Tertiary path
⑦ Activity area
⑧ Parking area
⑨ Park administration and restrooms
⑩ Park entry
⑪ Street

Figure 2.14. Park circulation hierarchy

· Install warning signs where pedestrian pathways intersect with bicycle routes and vehicular roads.

· Clearly mark pedestrian pathways.

· Locate pedestrian entrances near crosswalks outside the green space.

· Locate pedestrian entrances near public transport stations or stops to encourage and facilitate alternative modes of travel.

· Provide pathways that offer direct access to play areas, restrooms, and sports fields.

· Provide textured paving to discourage skateboarding near children's play areas and restroom buildings.

Bicycle

· Provide bicycle path connections to encourage and facilitate bicycle travel to and within the green space.

· Separate bicycle routes from pedestrian pathways and vehicular traffic where possible.

· Mark bicycle routes clearly.

Vehicular

· Locate vehicular entries to be compatible with roads outside the green space.

· Restrict automobiles to the perimeters of the green space, while providing access for vehicles required to deliver equipment for activities and events.

· Control vehicle speeds with signage, road plans, speed humps, textured decorative paving, traffic circles or roundabouts, and neckdowns/chokers (curb extensions).

· Provide separate entrances to parking areas and maintenance yards where possible.

· Provide access for large and heavy maintenance vehicles.

General

· Ensure paving design complies with engineer recommendations.

· Avoid abrupt and/or protruding edges or abrupt grade changes on all roads and pathways.

Recreational Facilities

The size and shape of a site can have a major influence on the types of recreation uses it can support. For example, a large and regular-shaped site may facilitate soccer or baseball fields, while a small and irregular-shaped site may facilitate basketball or tennis courts. In addition, the estimated area needed for a recreation facility should consider supporting features and/or amenities. This may include:

· Parking

· Restrooms

· Storage facilities

· Concession facilities

· Bleachers or other spectator areas

· Spillover noise and activity areas

· Surface drainage features

· Buffer zones

· Maintenance access areas

See Table 2.1 for the field dimensions of typical sports fields and courts.

The location and orientation of recreation fields should recognize and be sensitive to established surrounding conditions. Care must be taken to address potential conflicts with adjacent passive use areas, including children's play areas.

Table 2.1. Standard field dimensions and acreage for sports fields and courts

Sport	Field dimensions	Minimum area
Softball	60 ft (19 m) baseline, 275—300 ft (84—92 m) outfield	2 acres (0.8 hectares)
Baseball	90 ft (28 m) baseline, 350—380 ft (107—116 m) outfield	3 acres (1.2 hectares)
Soccer	225 x 330 ft (69 x 101 m) field dimension	1—2 acres (0.4—0.8 hectares)
Basketball	50 x 94 ft (15 x 29 m)	0.01 acres (0.004 hectares)
Tennis	78 x 36 ft (24 x 11 m)	0.06 acres (0.024 hectares)
Volleyball	30 x 59 ft (9 x 18 m)	0.05 acres (0.02 hectares)

Ball Fields

Field sizes vary from approximately three-quarters of an acre for a little league baseball field to approximately three acres for an adult baseball field.

· Provide a physical buffer or sufficient space for public safety, errant balls, spectator areas, and other ball field features.

· Orient the third base line with a north/south aspect wherever possible; some sites may require variations from this preferred orientation.

See Figure 2.15 for the standard layout of a typical baseball field and Figure 2.16 for the standard layout of a typical softball field.

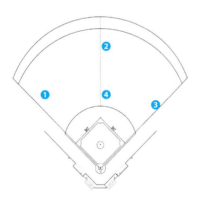

① 300 ft (91.4 m) min.–320 ft (97.5 m) max.
② 350 ft (106.7 m) min.–380 ft (115.8 m) max.
③ 300 ft (91.4 m) min.–320 ft (97.5 m) max.
④ Grass line

Figure 2.15. Baseball field—standard layout

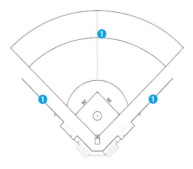

① 275 ft (83.8 m) min.–300 ft (91.4 m) max

Figure 2.16. Softball field—standard layout

Sports Fields

Many large athletic fields can be used for multiple purposes and sports that require areas of similar sizes and dimensions. Soccer fields vary greatly in size depending on the age and level of play and should be designed and laid out accordingly. A field for children six years of age and under is approximately 0.12 acres (0.05 hectares) in area while a field for adults can require nearly two acres (0.81 hectares). Additional area is also required for spectator areas, missed shots, and errant passes.

· Ensure all fields have a 2-percent maximum slope for positive drainage. Other drainage options should be considered if specific site conditions make this unattainable.

· Orient the long axis of a field with a north/south aspect wherever possible.

· Position multiple fields with 20 feet (6.1 meters) minimum space between them.

· Provide an area of 20 feet (6.1 meters) in width around the field's perimeter with no trees, berms, planters, sidewalks, or light fixtures.

See Figure 2.17 for the standard layout of a typical soccer field.

① 300 ft (91.4 m) max.,150 ft (45.7 m) min.
② 390 ft (118.9 m) max., 300 ft (91.4 m) min.
③ Marking to be 4—5 in (10—13 cm) wide
④ Penalty area
⑤ Goal, 8 ft (2.4 m) in height; 14 ft (4.3 m) in width; 5 ft (1.5 m) in depth
⑥ Corner mark

Figure 2.17. Soccer field—standard layout

Sports Courts

Basketball and Multi-use Courts

· Locate sports courts along the edges of the green space to maximize visibility and security.

· Incorporate a low berm or low-planted landscape buffer to separate courts from the street.

· Ensure all courts have a 1-percent maximum slope for positive drainage.

· Provide sports lighting.

· Consider surrounding land uses to reduce possible impacts from noise and sports lighting.

· Locate adult/teen activities away from small children's play areas and passive activity areas.

· Provide shaded spectator seating at the court perimeters.

· Position side-by-side courts with a minimum of 10 feet (3 meters) between them.

· Apply all court markings using a wear-resistant, colored substance.

· Orient the long axis of a court with a north/south aspect wherever possible.

See Figure 2.18 for the standard layout of a typical basketball court and Figure 2.19 for the standard layout of a typical volleyball court.

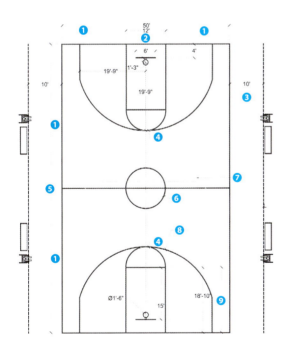

① Inside line
② Outside line
③ 10 ft (3 m) of unobstructed space
④ 6 ft (1.8m) radius (R6')
⑤ 84 ft (25.6 m) maximum
⑥ 6 ft (1.8 m) radius outside line
⑦ Full court striped for volleyball in yellow
⑧ 20.75 ft (6.3 m) radius outside line
⑨ To center of circle

Figure 2.18. Basketball court—standard layout over volleyball court

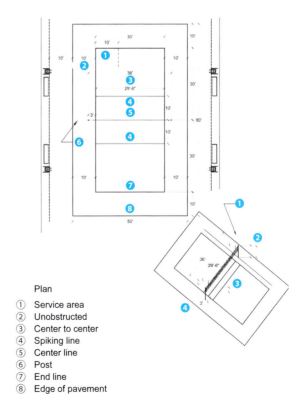

Plan
① Service area
② Unobstructed
③ Center to center
④ Spiking line
⑤ Center line
⑥ Post
⑦ End line
⑧ Edge of pavement

Isometric showing net
① Post, 8.3 ft (2.5 m) maximum
② 8 ft (2.4 m) men
③ 7.3 ft (2.2 m) women
④ 3 ft (90 cm) net

Figure 2.19. Volleyball court—standard layout

Tennis Courts

· Orient the long axis of a court with a north/south aspect wherever possible.

· Position side-by-side courts with a minimum of 12 feet (3.7 meters) between them.

· Position end-to-end courts a minimum of 21 feet (6.4 meters) apart.

· Apply an appropriate slip-resistant surfacing to the court.

· Apply all markings to the playing surface using a wear-resistant, colored substance.

· Provide vented windscreen fabric on perimeter fencing.

· Provide a practice wall (without side walls) on one side or end of the tennis court.

See Figure 2.20 for the standard layout of a typical tennis court.

Skate Parks

Skating has a younger-than-average target demographic and participants compete against others as well as environmental obstacles and challenges. There are a variety of styles of skate parks with varying degrees of difficulty, including above-ground skate parks that offer the convenience of installing moveable skate elements, and in-ground skate parks that offer greater challenge and a higher degree of flow or movement between elements.

· Ensure skate surfaces are smooth concrete with a tubular steel perimeter fence enclosing the area.

· Provide a vehicular maintenance pathway and double-gate entry for access.

· Provide shaded spectator bleachers and a drinking fountain.

· Capture and manage stormwater runoff from sloped surfaces.

· Provide sports lighting sensitive to spillover into the surrounding neighborhood.

· Locate skate parks away from small children's activities.

· Provide a pedestrian pathway linking the skate park to the primary circulation path.

Active Recreation Amenities

Fitness zones are outdoor facilities designed with kinetic exercise equipment that can be used for physical activity.

· Provide accessibility for people with and without disabilities.

· Provide exercise apparatus for people with and without disabilities.

· Provide durable and vandal-resistant equipment appropriate for teenagers and adults of all fitness levels.

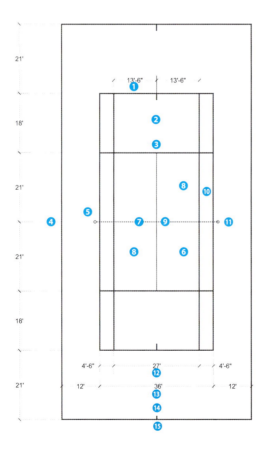

① Base line		⑨ Center service line	
② Back court		⑩ Alley line	
③ Service line		⑪ Side line	
④ Side screen		⑫ Singles	
⑤ Post		⑬ Doubles	
⑥ Right service court		⑭ Center mark	
⑦ Net fore		⑮ Back screen	
⑧ Left service court			

Figure 2.20. Tennis court—standard layout

Children's Play Areas

Playgrounds

Children's playgrounds fall into two age group classifications: preschool children aged two to four years old and school children aged five to twelve years old.

· Provide a suggested area of 2,500 square feet (233 square meters) for preschool children's playgrounds, and a suggested area of 5,000 square feet (465 square meters) for school children's playgrounds.

· Provide a suggested area of 7,000 square feet (650 square meters) for composite playgrounds that cater to preschool and school children. Functionally and physically separate play structures with barriers and space to ensure play patterns do not interfere with one another.

· Site play areas with safety in mind, maintaining space and implementing a buffer between play areas and vehicular traffic, ball fields, and sports courts, as illustrated in Figure 2.21.

· Develop natural barriers or features to segregate play areas from conflicting or incompatible uses.

· Develop playgrounds that enrich children's developmental needs, including physical, social, creative, cognitive, and sensory experiences. This may include equipment that encourages:

-Swinging

-Spinning

-Climbing

-Balancing

-Sliding

-Touching

-Crawling

-Imagination

-Adventure

-Problem solving

· Provide shaded seating, such as benches under trees or canopies, in close proximity to play areas for adult supervision.

· Link play areas to open space.

· Provide unobstructed lines of sight between separate play areas for ease of supervision.

· Shade playground equipment with freestanding or attached structures.

· Locate restrooms within 100 feet (30.5 meters) of play areas and within clear lines of sight from play areas.

· Provide water fountains in close proximity to play areas.

· Incorporate equipment and apparatus for use by children with and without disabilities.

· Scale equipment and apparatus to the size of intended users.

· Clearly mark each playground entrance with signage that states the age appropriateness of the play equipment and recommendations for adult supervision.

Equipment

· Ensure playground equipment and design meets safety guidelines and standards.

· Ensure playground equipment is durable and routinely maintained.

· Incorporate a theme or concept for the playground where possible.

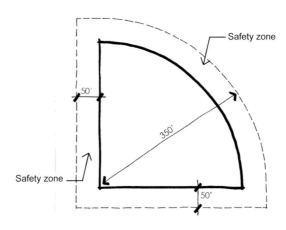

Figure 2.21. Buffer between children's play areas and ball fields

Splash Pads

A splash pad is a water playground that has little or no standing water.

· Shade splash pads with shade sails to ensure surface water temperatures do not get too hot.

· Shade benches outside splash pads for parental observation.

· Install corrosive-resistant fences around splash pads for safety.

· Determine wind directions and assess the possible impacts of overspray onto vegetation within the vicinity of splash pads.

· Minimize the accumulation of leaf debris or grass clippings around splash pads to reduce water filtration issues.

· Incorporate strategic design features to discourage skateboarding.

· Design facilities for use by people with and without disabilities.

· Provide restrooms with warm water service in the proximity of splash pads.

· Provide a combination of in-ground spray orifices and stainless steel upright equipment as sources of the spray features.

Passive Recreation Areas

A passive recreation area may be defined as an open, unobstructed space used for non-programmed recreation activities.

Open Play Areas

· Locate open play areas in spaces unobstructed by trees to support activities such as throwing a ball or Frisbee, or flying a kite.

· Locate open play areas adjacent to picnic and children's play areas.

· Provide shade trees at the perimeter of open play areas.

· Provide regulatory signs that describe permitted uses within open play areas.

Picnic Areas

· Provide picnic tables a minimum of 6 feet (1.8 meters) long.

· Cluster picnic tables to accommodate small groups (25 to 50 people) and large groups (50 to 100 people).

· Shade picnic areas with trees or freestanding or attached structures.

· Provide lighting in picnic areas.

· Provide an appropriate ratio of barbecue grills and trash receptacles to picnic tables.

· Provide a counter top equipped with a sink and faucet.

· Provide signs with picnic area names or numbers for identification and rental purposes.

· Provide restrooms and drinking fountains within 150 feet (45.7 meters) of picnic areas.

· Ensure all picnic areas, picnic tables, and associated amenities are accessible for people with and without disabilities.

Furnishings

· Ensure all park furnishings are sustainable products and effectively minimize negative environmental impacts over their life cycle. This may include products that are made from natural and recycled materials, are durable and long lasting, conserve energy and water, reduce greenhouse gas emissions, use unbleached or chlorine-free manufacturing processes, and use wood from sustainable harvested forests.

· Design and implement furnishings, including signage, light fixtures, drinking fountains, trash receptacles, and benches, with consistency in order to create a distinct character for the green space.

· Securely anchor all furnishings to the ground or a wall.

· Deter skateboarders with skateboarding stops on edges of concrete benches and low seat walls.

Benches

· Install benches at key locations throughout the green space including at the entrance, at regular intervals along the main circulation path, at vistas and outlooks, and at all play areas and activity areas.

· Position benches to be singular or grouped to support solitary activities and gatherings.

· Situate benches with the back toward a wall, landscape planting, or trees to increase a sense of user security.

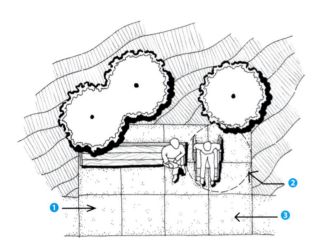

① Wheelchair accessible surface materials
② 2.5 ft (75cm) radius
③ Pathway

Figure 2.22. Park bench with adjacent seating for people with disabilities

· Set benches back from circulation paths of travel to reduce pedestrian obstructions.

· Position benches to maximize shade opportunities in the summer and sun exposure in the winter.

· Provide benches to accommodate people with and without disabilities, as illustrated in Figure 2.22.

· Provide benches designed with a center armrest or center break to discourage sleeping.

· Position benches to be freestanding or integrated into walls or other design features.

Natural Furnishings

· Natural design features can be used for various functional purposes throughout a green space.

· Use boulders to define pedestrian or vehicular edges and boundaries.

· Incorporate boulders for casual seating and natural decorative effects.

Park Signage

· Mark entrances, areas, and green space features with clearly identifiable and readable signage.

· Design all signage with a consistent look.

· Provide an information board and/or kiosk to promote events and activities, and to display a map of the green space and its features.

Bicycle Racks

· Locate bicycle racks near amenities and where they are accessible by vehicular roadways.

Trash Receptacles

· Provide an adequate number of trash receptacles near all parking areas, entrances to buildings and restrooms, playgrounds, picnic areas, spectator areas, and at active recreation areas.

· Design trash receptacles to match all furnishings.

Landscaping

Planted Area

Landscape design must be sensitive and appropriate for the project site to minimize disruption to existing plant habitats. Use climate-appropriate plants to support the design intent and plan planting designs that incorporate biodiversity and water conservation.

Design Considerations

· Use only non-invasive plants that are nursery grown or legally harvested.

· Select plant materials that promote and support the regional identity of the green space location.

· Include low-maintenance natural and naturalized areas that may accommodate recreation activities such as picnicking, biking, and walking.

· Incorporate and protect naturally occurring landscape features such as tree groves, dry streambeds, rock features, and earth forms to enhance the natural character of the site.

· Use native species in natural settings such as on special-use sites and corridors, graded slopes in environmentally sensitive areas, riparian areas, wetland and watershed rehabilitation areas, wildlife habitat restoration areas, post-fire rehabilitation areas, and demonstration gardens.

· Preserve all trees designated as natural resources.

· Plant trees and other greenery around buildings to create microclimates, lower energy consumption, and reduce costs associated with indoor energy needs.

· Reduce the heat island effect generated from the reflection of hardscape surfaces by shading pathways, roofs, and parking areas with trees or vegetated structures.

· Plant medium canopy trees with non-invasive roots in areas adjacent to paved circulation paths and parking to provide shade, reduce heat build-up, and minimize glare.

· Locate vegetated bioswales outside of active recreation areas for stormwater management.

· Control and remove invasive plant species to minimize damage to local plant ecosystems.

· Mitigate potential fire hazards in fire-threatened areas.

· Ensure new and existing planting designs are complementary for continuity.

· Select and locate shrubs with consideration for their function and size at full maturity to minimize pruning and to maintain the natural characteristics of the selected shrubs.

· Ensure landscape materials do not obstruct visibility into and out of the green space where security may be an issue.

· Ensure planter areas have low maintenance and hardy plants.

· Select turf types that require less mowing and water.

· Grade turf areas no steeper than a 5:1 slope for easier mowing.

· Separate planted areas from turf areas.

· Provide root barrier protection for trees planted 5 feet (1.5 meters) or less from hardscape surfaces.

· Use dense landscaping, screen walls, berming and/or mounding to screen service, loading, maintenance and storage areas, and trash enclosures.

· Identify the most appropriate areas to include shrubs and ground cover plantings to maximize water conservation. Create a

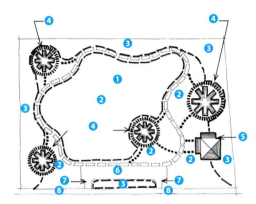

1. Active sports areas (turf required)
2. Passive recreation areas (turf typically required)
3. Potential planted areas (remaining non-pedestrian areas suitable for planted areas)
4. Activity area
5. Park administration and restroom
6. Parking area
7. Park entry
8. Street

Figure 2.23. Parkland activity use analysis example

"parkland activity use analysis" as illustrated in Figure 2.23; it is a useful tool for determining which areas are the most suitable for shrubs and ground covers. This analysis identifies:

1. Active sports areas (turf required)

2. Passive recreation areas (turf typically required)

3. Potential planted areas (remaining non-pedestrian areas suitable for planted areas)

Plant Material

Develop a planting plan with landscaping guidelines to help achieve water conservation and design objectives for the green space. Landscaping guidelines should be established for the ecology and biodiversity of a green space.

The following is an example of landscaping guidelines appropriate to parks in Los Angeles, California, where drought may be an issue. These guidelines will vary for other regions, climates, and environments around the world and should be adapted appropriately. The guidelines include three plant lists:

· Preferred plant list—potable water

· Preferred plant list—recycled water

· Do not use plant list

In relation to parks in Los Angeles, the "preferred plant list" consists of drought-tolerant plant material known to perform well in a green space environment. The "do not use plant list" consists of plant material considered inappropriate. These plants may be invasive, short lived, delicate, require intensive maintenance, require greater than moderate water usage, or provide a strong attractant to bees.

The guidelines recommend designers verify the approximate date the green space will be connected to a recycled-water mainline. If the park is more than two years away from connection to recycled water, the "potable water" plant list will assist designers in preparing an appropriate plant palette. If the park is within two years of connection to recycled water, the "recycled water" plant list will assist designers in preparing a successful plant palette.

Categories of Water Needs

The guidelines advise designers to group plant materials with similar water requirements into common hydrozones, and plant species are evaluated as needing high, moderate, low, and very low amounts of irrigation water. These categories are expressed as a percentage of reference evapotranspiration (ETo) and quantitatively defined as follows:

High (H) = 70%-90% ETo

Moderate (M) = 40%-60% ETo

Low (L) = 10%-30% ETo

Very Low (VL) = <10% ETo

- = Inappropriate

? = Unknown

Irrigation

· Design irrigations systems to prevent runoff, drainage from low head, overspray, and other similar inefficient conditions where irrigation water flows onto non-targeted areas, such as adjacent properties, non-irrigated areas, paved areas, roadways, or structures.

· Design irrigation head spacing to provide 120 percent coverage.

· Design irrigation systems to allow for seasonal water amounts.

· Determine and reference relevant information such as soil type and infiltration rate.

Utilities

· Utilize solar technology and/or LED in all green space buildings, parking areas, security lighting, and recreation facility lighting wherever possible.

· Select proper equipment and system controls for efficient use of energy.

Security Lighting

· Use solar lighting wherever possible.

· Provide exterior security lighting at parking areas, restrooms buildings, and along circulation routes.

· Use high-efficiency lighting with low cut-off angles and down lighting.

· Use reflective-type lighting fixtures to reduce or eliminate glare.

· Do not allow direct-beam exterior lighting at the property line.

Telecommunication Systems

· Incorporate telecommunication systems in green space facility buildings, including Internet access and multiple telephone lines.

Smoke/Fire Detection Systems

· Follow all governing agency codes and requirements for proper smoke and fire detection systems.

The Community-based Reinvention of Teleki Square

Location: Budapest, Hungary
Area: 3.5 acres (1.4 hectares)
Completion date: 2014
Landscape design: Újirány / New Directions Landscape Architects
Photography: Újirány / New Directions Landscape Architects, Tamas Bujnovszky, Tibor Vermes, Gyula Nyari, Attila Glázer
Client: Municipality of Józsefváros

Teleki Square in Józsefváros is one of the oldest squares in Budapest and today is located in one of the city's most disadvantaged neighborhoods. The Community-based Reinvention of Teleki Square saw it transformed from a barren and unsafe place to a functional urban green space.

The community-based planning process encouraged nearby residents to participate in developing the design of the park. A series of 12 workshops, an onsite exhibition, and a Facebook page enabled residents to imagine and contribute to a better future vision for themselves. Residents also formed the Teleki Square Association to continue their involvement in the management and ongoing improvements of the green space.

Teleki Square has a triangular shape and its layout is structured by a circulation system that divides the green space into smaller triangular-shaped areas. The forum and event space are located nearest to the city and serve as meeting points. Park users can plant flowers in the ornamental garden, and play chess, read a book, or relax in the quiet and shaded resting area. There is a children's garden and a teen corner, as well as designated spaces for dogs.

Permeable pavements and paved areas with a 2-percent gradient transfer rainwater toward green areas such as gullies and trees. Soil is recessed at the edges of paved and green areas to prevent mud on the pavement.

1 Ornamental garden with sunbathing lawn in background
2 Seating in ornamental garden
3 Visualization of ornamental garden

Site plan

① Reading garden
② Dog park for large dogs
③ Information panels
④ Stage
⑤ Event area
⑥ Forum vestibule
⑦ Main entrance
⑧ Large stairs
⑨ Daytime forum
⑩ Sunbathing lawn
⑪ Ornamental garden
⑫ Area for preschool children
⑬ Children's garden
⑭ Play garden
⑮ Hilly garden
⑯ Soccer ground
⑰ Teen corner
⑱ Dog park for small dogs

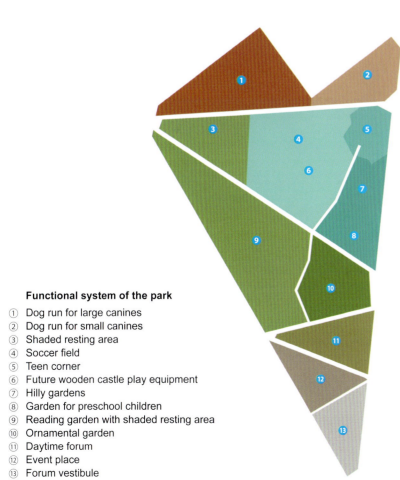

Functional system of the park

① Dog run for large canines
② Dog run for small canines
③ Shaded resting area
④ Soccer field
⑤ Teen corner
⑥ Future wooden castle play equipment
⑦ Hilly gardens
⑧ Garden for preschool children
⑨ Reading garden with shaded resting area
⑩ Ornamental garden
⑪ Daytime forum
⑫ Event place
⑬ Forum vestibule

1   Crushed stone path in ornamental garden
2   Water feature in ornamental garden
3   Visualization of hilly garden
4   Visualization of playground for preschool children
5   Playground for children of different ages
6   Teenagers enjoying the revitalized park

1 Information panels at left and sunbathing lawn at right
2 Large stair at the daytime forum doubles as stage seating
3 Visualization of information area and daytime forum
4 Picturesque trees in the reading garden
5 Pathway through the reading garden

1 Cherry trees and information panels
2 Playground for preschool children
3 Pallets in the teenage area; painted by residents

Mary Bartelme Park

Location: Chicago, United States
Area: 2.4 acres (0.97 hectares)
Completion date: 2012
Landscape design: site design group, ltd.
Photography: Bradley Swanson, site design group, ltd.
Client: Chicago Park District

Mary Bartelme Park is a contemporary pocket park that occupies the site of a former infirmary in the West Loop, Chicago. In recent years the West Loop has transitioned from being a dangerous and dilapidated industrial warehouse district to becoming one of the fastest growing neighborhoods in Chicago and home to numerous upscale residences and trendy restaurants. However, with rapid growth came a lack of green space, which spurred the development of Mary Bartelme Park.

The park is situated on a single city block surrounded by commercial and residential buildings and it combines a sense of history with sustainable design practices. An enclosed seating area and contemplative garden space feature terracotta artifacts salvaged from the demolished infirmary building. Weathering-steel retaining walls surround the garden and pay homage to the former industrial use of the site and neighborhood.

River Birch trees and custom egg-shaped benches mark the southeast entrance. A fully accessible playground at the northeast corner is composed of recycled rubber surfacing, custom-designed bridges, slides, stepping pods, and climbing structures, and is a popular stop for families with small children. The playground is designed to provide inventive, exploratory play experiences and physical challenges for children aged from two to twelve years old and it caters to children with a range of physical and cognitive abilities and disabilities.

A 7-foot-high (2.1-meter-high) mound along the northern edge of the park offers views of the green space and skyline. A secondary mounded open lawn forms the central spine of the park, which provides ample space for community activities such as holiday parades, movies, and recreation. The sunken dog park has anti-microbial and short-bladed artificial canine turf. It also has an oversized dog bowl, as well as ramps, steps, and seat walls for dog owners to rest.

The green space has served as a successful design project for the Chicago Park District, which has since begun implementing its sustainable solutions throughout many of its 580 parks. The project team used zero infrastructure for stormwater treatment. All runoff is directed towards the primary intersecting paths that are made of permeable pavers. Water infiltrates into a leach field located under a central berm below the surface where it is cleansed and infiltrated into the ground. Photocatalytic smog-eating pavers are installed below the entrance gateway to the park to alleviate the urban heat island effect and reduce air pollution.

1 Bird's-eye view of the park
2 Approaching the park from the southeast, River Birch trees line the entry along with a cluster of custom-built egg-shaped benches

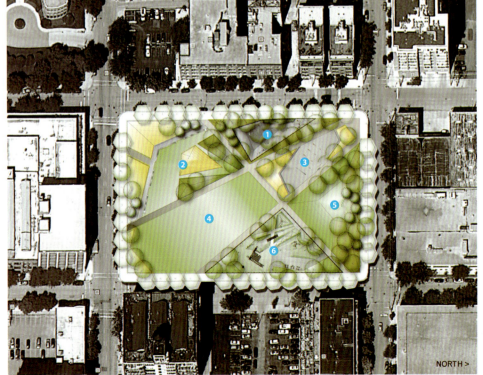

Site plan
① Dog friendly area
② Contemplative garden
③ Gateway fountain
④ Open lawn
⑤ Viewing mound
⑥ Sculpted playground

NORTH >

Stormwater axonometric diagram

① Dry well
② Leach field located below the surface
③ Permeable paving

1

1 Playground provides inventive, exploratory play experiences and physical challenges for preschool and school children, and accommodates for people with physical and cognitive disabilities
2 Gateway fountain is framed by ornamental and native plants that provide year-round interest
3 Primary paths are made of permeable paving. Runoff from across the site is infiltrated and directed into a leach field located under a central berm, where the stormwater is cleansed and infiltrated into the ground
4 Fully accessible playground contains custom play structures and complex topography that allows multiple age groups to play together
5 Planting design takes advantage of Chicago's full range of seasons

Kapellparken–A Waterfront Park

Location: Västerås, Sweden
Area: 1.2 acres (0.5 hectares)
Completion date: 2012
Landscape design: Sweco Architects AB
Photography: Sweco Architects AB, Tim Meier
Client: MUAB

Kapellparken–A Waterfront Park is a bright and open space in Västerås, Sweden, and it draws on the characteristic nature of Lake Mälaren. The park is a robust space, adaptable for present and future demands, and it has proved popular with local residents who appreciate the sunny seating areas.

Planting and a water feature are concentrated to the formal axis, which serves as a link between the commercial square and visitor marina. Low shrubs and perennials are planted to create intimate spaces while heavier planting of Sea Buckthorn beech is concentrated in areas close to the park boulevard.

The south-facing ground has sunny spots with views of the water and protection against the elements. A wooden palisade fence runs alongside the boulevard and the wharf provides further protection against the wind. Small seating areas are like wooden jetties, and a retaining wall and stepped seating highlight the level differences.

The stormwater management system does not use traditional drains and pipes. Rather, permeable materials allow water to infiltrate, and gaps in the weathering-steel edging redirect excess water from gravel walkways to grass and planting areas where it infiltrates for retention and filtering. The lower part of the park has a shallow bowl-shaped depression for water to stand for a short period of time in heavy rainfall.

1 Kapellparken is a bright and open waterfront space
2 Benches overlook the wharf and marina
3 Lower grasses surround a spine of Calamagrostis x acutiflora 'Karl Foerster;' Sedum spurium 'Brilliant' in foreground; Salix alba 'Tristis' in background
4 Planting inspired by characteristic nature of Lake Mälaren

Kapellparken early plan

① The lagoon
② Marin planting
③ Boardwalk
④ Sidewalk
⑤ Turning space

Kapellparken section ground modeling

Neisse Waterfront Park, Görlitz

Location: Görlitz, Germany
Area: 3.7 acres (1.5 hectares)
Completion date: 2013
Landscape design: Rehwaldt Landschaftsarchitekten
Photography: Rehwaldt Landschaftsarchitekten
Client: City of Görlitz, Agency of Urban Planning

Neisse Waterfront Park, Görlitz, is situated along the Neisse riverside and offers extensive views across the river while flattened riverbanks enable park users safe access to the water.

"Tuchbahnen"—the spread of fabric—is the central theme of the project. It is inspired by the textile industry that formerly occupied the site and it informs the design and identity of the green space. For example, large embossed floor panels quote the classic patterns of industrial weaving, and stretches of bright concrete pathways recall cloth laid out for bleaching. These pathways also absorb rainwater to regulate local climate and purify the air.

Different types of trees at the north and south ends of the green space foster a different atmosphere in each area. Hardwoods, such as oak trees, are in the south, while birch trees are in the north. The seating furniture is inspired by the quiet flow of the river and the adjacent longitudinal landscape, and benches are positioned like long timbers logs, offering visitors different views of the landscape.

1-2 Visitors relax on benches alongside the riverbank

Site plan

Bird's-eye view

Neisse Bank

Promenade
Former textile mill
Textile park

Wetlands

Site plan 1/2000

① St. Peter Church
② Old town bridge
③ Promenade
④ Culture quarter former textile mill
⑤ Neisse
⑥ Textile park
⑦ Park
⑧ Pedestrian bridge
⑨ Park extension
⑩ Plaza
⑪ Neisse wetland
⑫ Bank path
⑬ Connecting city park Neisse wetland
⑭ City park
⑮ City hall

Textile line

Former textile mill

Textile line

Former textile mill

Trees

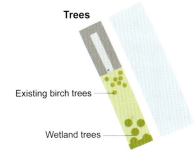

Existing birch trees

Wetland trees

Existing birch

Culture quarter textile mill

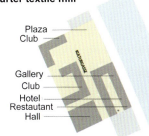

Plaza
Club

Gallery
Club
Hotel
Restautant
Hall

Gastronomy

Section AB 1/200

1 Pathways absorb rainwater to regulate local climate and purify the air
2 Wooden benches are positioned like long timbers logs

64

Visualization

Texitile lines

Comfortable path

Jumping field

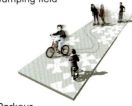

Parkour

Concrete surface (blasted)

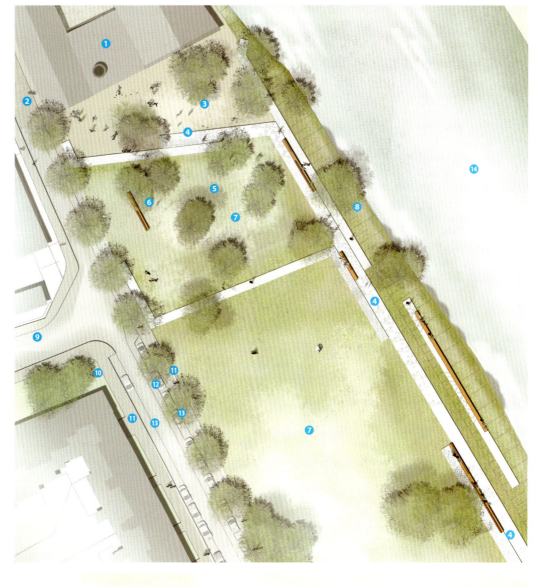

Site plan 1/200

① Former textile mill
② Culture lane
③ Sun plaza
④ Textile lines with weaving patterns
⑤ Birch trees
⑥ River benches
⑦ Meadow
⑧ Bank slope
⑨ Bergstrab
⑩ Garden
⑪ Sidewalk
⑫ Cycle path
⑬ Parking
⑭ Neisse

1 Sun plaza in front of residential buildings
2 Detail of "Tuchbahnen" (spread of fabric)
3-4 Decorative patterns on the ground
5 Sun plaza provides a large green space for play and relaxation
6 Riverbank recreational area

Akasya Acibadem Central Park

Location: Istanbul, Turkey
Area: 2.2 acres (0.9 hectares)
Completion date: 2014
Landscape design: SdARCH Trivelli & Associati and Alhadeff Architects
Photography: SdARCH Trivelli & Associati
Client: Akasya Acibadem

Akasya Acibadem Central Park is the green center of a new urban development that has seen a network of roads, residential housing, and shopping mall built in Akasya, Istanbul. The landscape architects designed the public area in front of the main entrance of Akasya Acibadem shopping mall as a place where visitors and shoppers can rest or spend time with other people.

The mall is encircled by a ring of roads and the shape of the garden shares the same rounded lines and circular shapes, with natural pathways conceived in many types of grass, herbs, and shrubs. There are 293 trees of 15 different species, reflecting the Mediterranean vegetation, and 47 species of shrubs and flowers. Rows of same-species trees, such as olive, pine, oak, birch, and willow, demarcate the circular multicolored areas.

Different spaces allow people to carry out various activities; some spaces are more private, such as the lowered pond, while others are more social, such as the theater, fountains and places where parents can play with their children. The children's playground is on a small hill with slides, boulders, mazes, and rubber hooks for climbing. Shows, concerts, and other cultural and recreational activities take place at the open-air theater during the day and evening. A small pond and a large fountain at the park entrance are designed to amaze visitors with numerous water jets that dance to music.

Energy efficiency is achieved through rainwater harvesting and greywater (recycled water, used for landscape irrigation) for pools and gardens. Levostab 99 is used for pathways; it is a paving stabilizer that has soil line properties surpassing asphalt and concrete-based pavements.

Site plan

Section A-A

Section B-B

1 Lush trees and vegetation
2 Green hills for children to play
3 Pond and water play area
4 Swings for children to play on
5 Colorful planting
6 Gardens share the rounded lines and circular shapes with
  natural pathways conceived in many types of grass, herbs, and shrubs

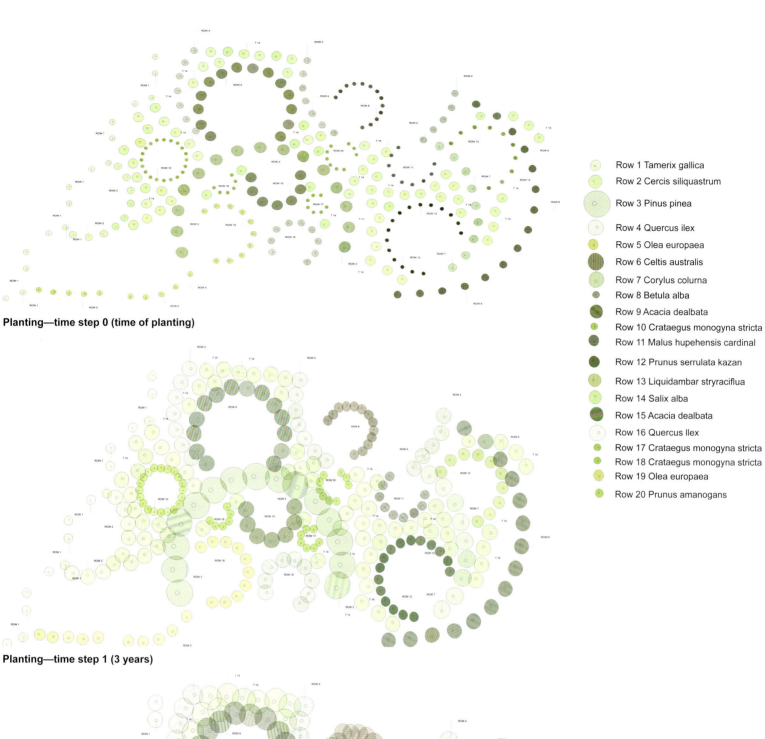

Planting—time step 0 (time of planting)

Row 1 Tamerix gallica
Row 2 Cercis siliquastrum
Row 3 Pinus pinea
Row 4 Quercus ilex
Row 5 Olea europaea
Row 6 Celtis australis
Row 7 Corylus colurna
Row 8 Betula alba
Row 9 Acacia dealbata
Row 10 Crataegus monogyna stricta
Row 11 Malus hupehensis cardinal
Row 12 Prunus serrulata kazan
Row 13 Liquidambar stryraciflua
Row 14 Salix alba
Row 15 Acacia dealbata
Row 16 Quercus Ilex
Row 17 Crataegus monogyna stricta
Row 18 Crataegus monogyna stricta
Row 19 Olea europaea
Row 20 Prunus amanogans

Planting—time step 1 (3 years)

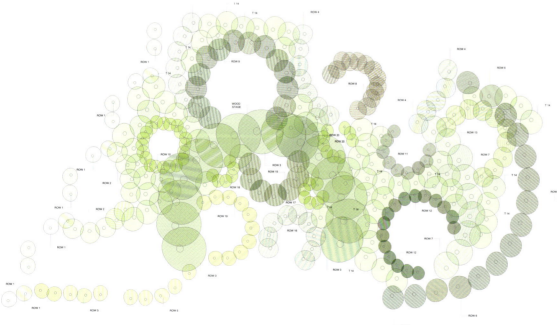

Planting—time step 2 (10 years)

1 There are 15 different species of trees and 47 different shrubs/flower
2 Open-air theater surrounded by vegetation

The Liberation Park

Location: Uden, Netherlands
Area: 12.4 acres (5 hectares)
Completion date: 2011
Landscape design: HOUTMAN+SANDER Landscape Architecture - André Houtman en Margriet Sander
Photography: HOUTMAN+SANDER, STUDIO TERP
Client: City Government of Uden

The Liberation Park is located in Uden, a small city in southern Netherlands. The development of the park saw a valuable but unused and undefined open green space transformed into the main leisure place for nearby residents.

The design resituated the large existing trees but added more landscape value and diversity to the experience of the park and its potential land use. The relocation of 58 large lime trees established a spine along the edge of the redeveloped park—Lime Lane—which connects the center of the city with its surrounding suburbs.

Hedges demarcate four large oval-shaped areas that are designed to suggest possible uses of the smaller and larger spaces. Shrubs and plants enrich the park's ecological value for smaller animals, and the selection of trees with seasonal leaf changes and blossoms are intended to enhance seasonal recognition and the overall experience of the landscape.

There is reduced need for intense stormwater management because of the amount of open water in the neighborhood and low-density urban development. Pavements are made of asphalt and permeable gravel and rainwater is directly drained to the trees and plants to prevent dehydration. A drainage system underneath the festival field provides a year-round playground.

1 Playground and soccer field
2 Lime Lane for walking and cycling

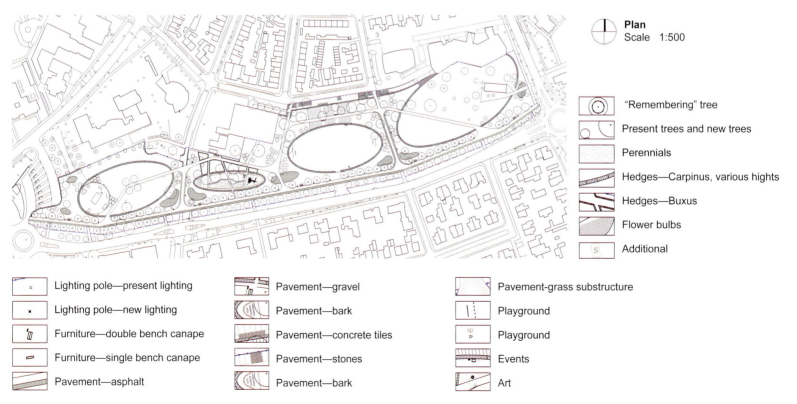

Plan
Scale   1:500

"Remembering" tree

Present trees and new trees

Perennials

Hedges—Carpinus, various hights

Hedges—Buxus

Flower bulbs

Additional

Lighting pole—present lighting

Lighting pole—new lighting

Furniture—double bench canape

Furniture—single bench canape

Pavement—asphalt

Pavement—gravel

Pavement—bark

Pavement—concrete tiles

Pavement—stones

Pavement—bark

Pavement-grass substructure

Playground

Playground

Events

Art

 Present trees

 Transplanted trees within project site

 New trees

Tree species

Cj Cercidiphyllum japonicum 18/20, chunk
Cs Cercis siliquastrum multitrunk, 2-3 trunks, 10 feet (3 meters), chunk
Ls Liquidambar styraciflua 18/20, chunk
Ns Nyssa sylvatica 18/20, chunk
Mk Magnolia kobus 18/20, chunk
Py Prunus x yedoensis 18/20, chunk
Tv Tilia vulgaris 20/25, chunk
Uk Cherry trees 18/20, chunk

Scale   1:1000

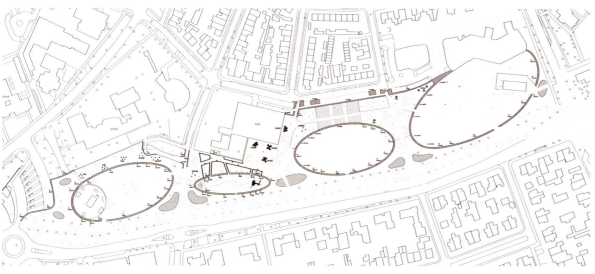

Scale   1:500

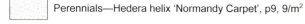

Perennials—Hedera helix 'Normandy Carpet', p9, 9/m²

Hedge—Buxus sempervirens, 30–40, double row, 10/m¹, 1.3 ft (40 cm)

Hedge—Carpinus betulus, 60–80, double row, 6/m¹, 2.6 ft (80 cm)

Hedges parking—Carpinus betulus, 60–80, 9/m², 2 ft (60 cm)

Hedge—Carpinus betulus, four rows, 3/m¹/row, 2.6–8.6 ft (80–200 cm)

Hedge—present

Hedge near church—Carpinus betulus, 100–125, double row, 6/m¹

Solitary shrubs—Amelanchier lamarckii

Solitary shrubs—Cornus kousa var. Chinensis

Solitary shrubs—Hamamelis mollis 'Boskoop'

Solitary shrubs—Hydrangea paniculata 'Grandiflora'

Flower bulbs—Narcissus 'Dutch Master,' 20/m²

Perennial garden

Special playground garden

1 View of playground and city center
2 Lime Lane with existing and transplanted lime trees

Detail—planting 1

① Present hedge—Carpinus betulus
② New hedge—Carpinus betulus, 100/125, double row, 3/m^1/row
③ Hedera helix 'Normandy Carpet' with shrubs
④ New trees
⑤ Existing asphalt
⑥ Present trees
⑦ Hedge—Buxus sempervirens
⑧ Hedera with solitary shrubs
⑨ Gravel—Gralux
⑩ Single bench canape, Erdi CA3100
⑪ Hedge—Carpinus betulus, width 4.9 ft (1.5 m)
⑫ New trees
⑬ Hedera helix 'Normandy Carpet'

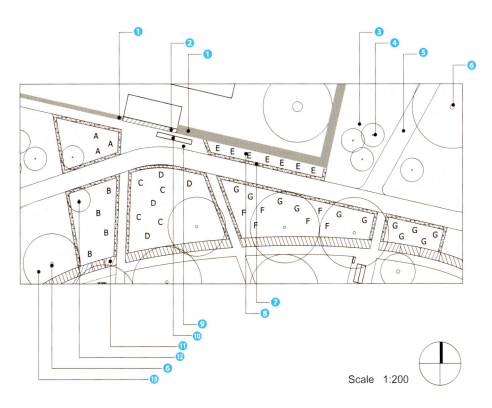

Scale   1:200

Number	Name	Size	nr/m²
A	Syringa vulgaris 'Olivier de Serres'	100–125	
B	Syringa vulgaris 'Madame Lemoine'	100–125	
C	Buddleja davidii 'Black Night'	pot	
D	Buddleja davidii 'White Profusion'	pot	
E	Hydrangea arborescens 'Grandiflora'	pot 3l	
F	Hydrangea paniculata 'Tardiva'	pot 3l	
G	Hydrangea serrata 'Bluebird'	pot 3l	
Hedge	Buxus sempervirens	30-40	Double row 10/m^1
Ground coverage	Hedera helix 'Normandy Carpet'	P9	9/m²

1 Perennial garden in bloom

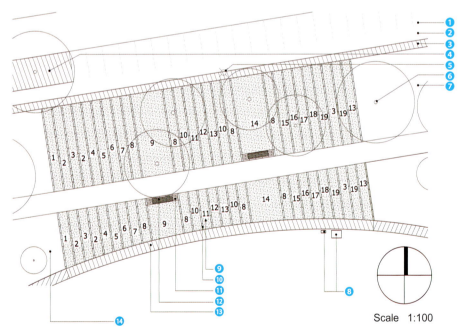

Scale 1:100

Number	Name	nr/m²	size
1	Leucanthemum 'Alaska'	8	P9
2	Alchemilla mollis	8	P9
3	Anemone x hybrida 'Honorine Jobert'	7	P9
4	Echinops ritro 'Veitch's Blue'	8	P9
5	Pennisetum alopecuroides	5	P9
6	Cimicifuga racemosa	7	P9
7	Coreopsis grandiflora 'Badengold'	8	P9
8	Dryopteris filix-mas	5	P9
9	Waldsteinia ternata	9	P9
10	Calamagrostis x acutifolia 'Karl Foerster'	7	P9
11	Acanthus mollis	5	P9
12	Ligularia dentata 'Othello'	7	P9
13	Aconitum carmichaelii 'Arendsii'	8	P9
14	Tiarella cordifolia	10	P9
15	Rudbeckia fulgida 'Goldsturm'	8	P9
16	Kirengeshoma palmata	8	P9
17	Hosta sieboldiana 'Elegans'	5	P9
18	Helenium 'Moerheim Beauty'	7	P9
19	Carex plantaginea	7	P9

Detail—planting 2

① Parking places—concrete stones black/gray
② Sidewalk—concrete tiles 1x1 ft (30x30 cm), gray
③ Hedge—Carpinus betulus, 2.6 ft (80 cm)
④ Hedge—Carpinus betulus, 2 ft (60 cm)
⑤ Lighting pole
⑥ Present trees
⑦ Hedera helix 'Normandy Carpet'

⑧ Electricity installation for events
⑨ Perennials, grasses, ferms
⑩ Path—Schellevis tile 2.3x7.8x39.3 in (6x20x100 cm), dark gray
⑪ Pavement—Schellevis tile 2.3x7.8x39.3 in (6x20x100 cm), dark gray
⑫ Single bench canape, Erdi CA3100
⑬ Hedge—Carpinus betulus, width 4.9 ft (1.5 m), several heights
⑭ Hedera helix 'Normandy Carpet'

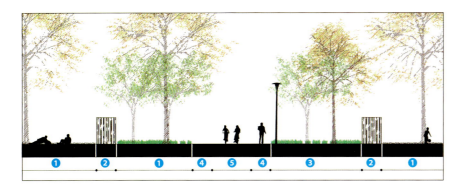

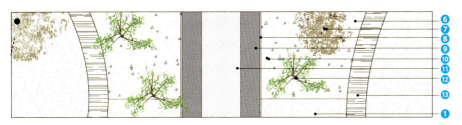

Section and detail 1   Scale 1:100

1. Grass
2. Hedge
3. Shrubs
4. Asphalt, black
5. Asphalt, gray
6. Hedera helix 'Normandy Carpet'
7. Present trees
8. Tile 100x200 mm, black
9. Stone layer on present asphalt
10. Lighting pole
11. Present asphalt
12. New trees—cherry trees
13. Hedge—Carpinus betulus, four rows, 6.5 ft (200 cm)

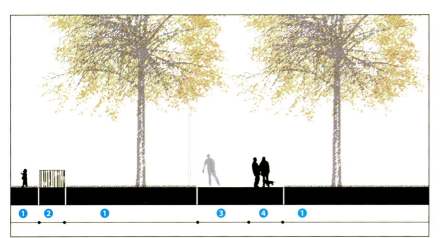

Section and detail 2   Scale 1:100

1. Grass
2. Hedge
3. Asphalt, gray
4. Asphalt, black
5. Transplanted lime trees
6. Hedge—Carpinus betulus, four rows, 2.6 ft (80 cm)
7. Present asphalt
8. Stone layer on present asphalt
9. Present lime trees

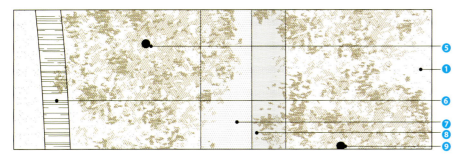

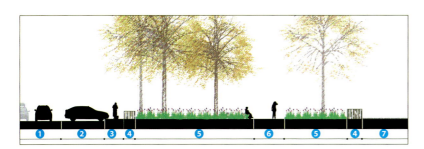

Section and detail 3   Scale 1:100

1. Road
2. Parking
3. Sidewalk
4. Hedge
5. Perennial garden
6. Asphalt
7. Grass
8. Perennials
9. Hedge—Carpinus betulus, double row, 2.6 ft (80 cm)
10. Tile 60x20x1000 mm, gray
11. Sidewalk—tile 1x1 ft (30x30 cm), gray
12. Tile 7x8x9x39 in (18x20x25x100 cm) ft, gray
13. Concrete stones, gray, 3 rows
14. Parking—concrete stones, black
15. Present trees
16. Electricity for events
17. Hedge—Carpinus betulus, four rows, 2.6 ft (80 cm)
18. Tiles 7.8x2.3 in (20x6 cm), dark gray, Schellevis
19. Present asphalt
20. Pavement—tiles 2.3x7.8x39.3 in (20x6x100 cm) dark gray, Schellevis
21. Single bench canape, Erdi CA3100

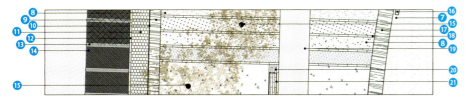

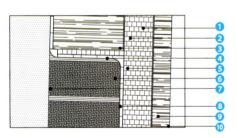

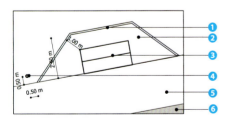

Detail 1—parking   Scale 1:100

1. Concrete tile 1x1 ft (30x30 cm), gray
2. Tile 2.3x7.8 in (6x20 cm), gray
3. Hedge—Carpinus betulus, 2 ft (60 cm)
4. Tile 1x1 ft (30x30 cm), gray
5. Tile Tile 7x8 in (18x20cm)
6. Concrete stones, black
7. Existing road
8. Concrete stones, gray
9. Tile 2.3x7.8in (6x20 cm), gray
10. Hedge—Carpinus betulus, 2.6 ft (80 cm)

Detail 2—bench Lime Lane   Scale 1:100

1. Tile 2.3x7.8in (6x20 cm), black
2. Pavement—asphalt black
3. Double bench ERDI CDZ3100
4. Lighting pole
5. Present asphalt
6. New asphalt-black

Detail 3—playground   Scale 1:100

1. Grass
2. Waste bin, Bammens Capitole
3. Steel edge 0.12 in (3 mm), Ferrx
4. Double bench canape, ERDI CDZ3100
5. Tile 2.3x7.8in (6x20 cm), black
6. Pavement gravel—Gralux
7. Sand playground

The Liberation Park, Uden   Scale 1:100

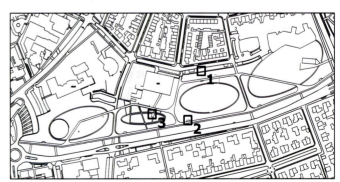

1 Cycling and pedestrian path
2 Perennial garden
3 Lane
4 Flowers in bloom

Skeppsmyreparken

Location: Stockholm, Sweden
Area: 2.5 acres (1 hectare)
Completion date: 2012
Landscape design: Land Arkitektur AB
Photography: Mauro Rongione
Client: Huddinge Municipality

Skeppsmyreparken underwent a complete transformation from worn-out and quiet green space to vibrant public park. It is one of the few larger green spots in Stuvsta, a relatively poor residential area on the outskirts of Stockholm. The project focused on creating a park that provides for a variety of users, ages, and interests.

The green space was first developed in the 1930s and the new design aimed to maintain its historic qualities while making distinct additions to cater to new needs and expectations. Two parallel alleys of birch trees remain from the original layout and mark a central axis for bicyclists and pedestrians. It improves access and communications through the park while also splitting the space into disconnected strips.

A circular grass field and two wooden structures add a new layer of connections and spatial qualities. Trees and stones define the shape of the field, while the field itself is free and open for spontaneous activities such as football, picnics, play, and rest. Wooden structures offer defined play areas on each side of the field and have integrated seating and lighting; one has a shipwreck theme as a play on the park's name. A pastel color scheme revitalizes the existing furniture and equipment, and a bronze sculpture by artist Amalia Årfelt features curious squirrels investigating the new space.

Tree species are chosen to improve ecological diversity and seasonal variation. The pavement allows water to permeate into the ground quickly and smoothly, and rainwater washes the ground, helping to keep it clean. The permeability of the pavement also facilitates the groundwater cycle and promotes the growth of the vegetation.

1 Wooden frame structure
2 Birch trees
3 Pathway provides access and communications through the park. Wooden structures offer defined play areas on each side

Bird's-eye view plan

Existing birch trees

Existing maple trees

New birch trees

Trees for seasonal variation

Gravel walkway with lighting

Bark path

Bench and table combined

Bench

Existing tree planting

🟢 Existing trees

Proposed tree planting

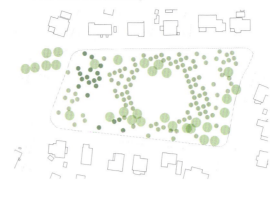

🟢 Preserved existing trees

● ● New trees

Existing walkways and entrances

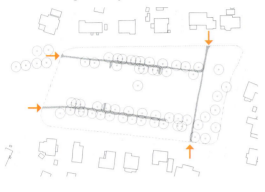

▬▬ Walkway

➜ Entrance

Proposed walkways and entrances

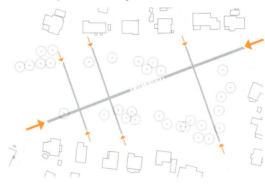

▬▬ Walkway

➜ Entrance

Existing surfaces and materials

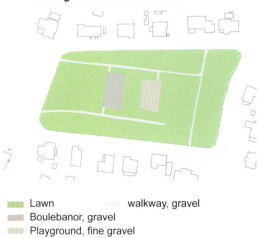

▨ Lawn ▨ walkway, gravel
▨ Boulebanor, gravel
▨ Playground, fine gravel

Proposed surfaces and materials

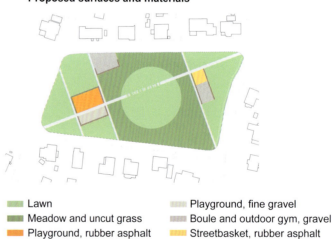

▨ Lawn ▨ Playground, fine gravel
▨ Meadow and uncut grass ▨ Boule and outdoor gym, gravel
▨ Playground, rubber asphalt ▨ Streetbasket, rubber asphalt

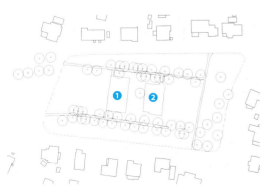

Existing activity areas

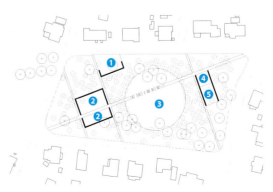

Proposed activity areas

① Boule
② Playground
③ Soccer, flea market, and picnic
④ Streetbasket
⑤ Outdoor gym

1-2 Circular glade with picnic benches

1   Pathway through the green space
2-4 Activity zone and picnic seating inside the wooden frame structure

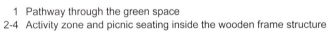

5-7 Skeppsmyreparken in summer

Märkische Promenade

Location: Blankenfelde-Mahlow, Germany
Area: 1.5 acres (0.6 hectares)
Completion date: 2014
Landscape design: gruppe F Landschaftsarchitekten
Photography: gruppe F Landschaftsarchitekten
Client: Municipality Blankenfelde-Mahlow

The development of Märkische Promenade was a community-based program in which landscape architects gruppe F collected the ideas and wishes of more than 100 public participants to involve them in the design concept. This was then transformed into a more detailed plan.

The linear park has been designed to connect different areas of the district and to provide a universally accessible and high-quality public green space for local residents of all ages, with areas for rest, play, and exercise spaced along the pathway. Existing trees influenced the placement of the light-colored asphalt pathways that are spacious enough for pedestrians, cyclists, wheelchair users, and skaters.

Decorative shrubs, perennial flowerbeds, and lawns are intended to improve residents' quality of life, and the different plants are selected for their behavioral characteristics and aesthetic appearance. For example, flowerbeds are in sun-exposed relaxation areas; evergreen plants improve the appearance of the park during winter; and groundcover is planted where lawn is impractical.

On-site drainage is achieved through a recess parallel to the pathway. The stormwater runs off to the sides via the convex surface and is cleaned and infiltrated in adjacent swales and raingardens. Additional subsurface infiltration trenches allow for faster infiltration of stormwater runoff in case of extreme rain events and in areas with little room for surface infiltration.

Site plan

① Shrub planting
② Maple
③ Linden
④ Oak
⑤ Beech
⑥ Hazel
⑦ Elm
⑧ Birch
⑨ Carprot
⑩ Jasmine
⑪ Walnut
⑫ Hazelnut
⑬ Fir
⑭ Bank
⑮ Adventitious roots
⑯ Forsythia
⑰ Cherry
⑱ Chestnut
⑲ Black cherry

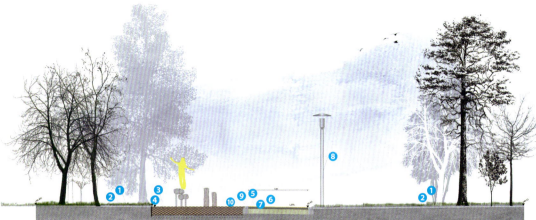

Section—path and playground elements

① Topsoil
② Pending floor
③ Safety flooring wood chips
④ Natural stone gravel
⑤ Rolled asphalt
⑥ Asphalt base
⑦ Base course
⑧ Pole-mounted light
⑨ Megalithic
⑩ Concrete foundation

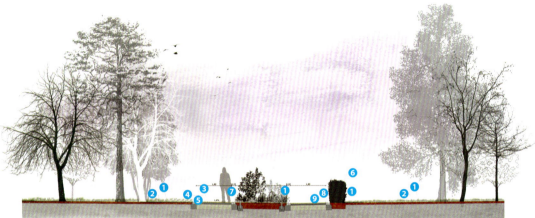

Section—path, flowerbed, and hedge

① Topsoil
② Pending floor
③ Rolled asphalt
④ Asphalt base
⑤ Base course
⑥ Hornbeam hedge
⑦ Tiergarten gitter (low border fence)
⑧ Megalithic
⑨ Concrete foundation

Section—path, seating area, and drainage ditch

① Topsoil
② Pending floor
③ Hornbeam hedge
④ Bench
⑤ Megalithic
⑥ Trough for stormwater infiltration
⑦ Rolled asphalt
⑧ Asphalt base
⑨ Base course

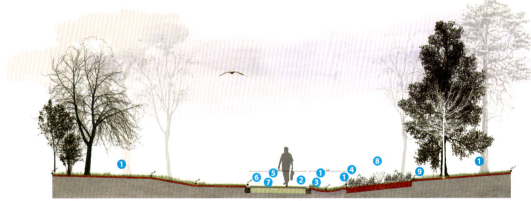

Section—path, drainage ditch, and flowerbeds

① Topsoil
② Megalithic
③ Trough for stormwater infiltration
④ Mulch cover
⑤ Rolled asphalt
⑥ Asphalt base
⑦ Base course
⑧ Planting perennials
⑨ Wood bed enclosure

96

1-2 Large paved seating area with central flowerbed
3 Play and exercise area with swing

1 Playground elements
2 Colored tarmac on main path
3 Detail of flowerbed
4 Metal grid for root protection on main path

Leise Park

Location: Berlin, Germany
Area: 3.7 acres (1.5 hectares)
Completion date: 2012
Landscape design: gruppe F Landschaftsarchitekten
Photography: gruppe F Landschaftsarchitekten
Client: Bezirksamt Pankow

The design of Leise Park was aimed at bringing long-lasting improvements to the Prenzlauer Berg neighborhood and the planning process involved an intensive participation initiative with residents, local institutions, and authorities. As a result, the new layout of the green space integrates much of its former appearance and qualities.

Leise Park incorporates traces of the old cemetery, which participants viewed as worth preserving, as well as the southern wilderness area that gives the park a partly wild and overgrown character. A narrow circulation path enables full access to the green space, and benches, wooden platforms, and playground features enrich the visitor experience.

Large areas of lawn and trees are beneficial for the local environment and contribute to a comfortable residential environment. Gravel pathways allow for some infiltration of stormwater, with surrounding green areas absorbing any remaining runoff.

① Graveyard relic
② Self-binding gravel

1 Aerial view
2 Central path with benches
3 Circle path with newly planted vegetation
4 Main path through the park

0,8

① ②

Elevation 2

① Graveyard relic
② Self-binding gravel

1 Re-used gravestones can be used as stepping stones
2 Lookout on playground
3 Play elements and lookout
4 Hammock for relaxation
5 Overgrown tombstones as relic of former graveyard

Alexandra Road Park

Location: London, England
Area: 4.2 acres (1.7 hectares)
Completion date: 2015
Landscape design: J & L Gibbons
Photography: J & L Gibbons, Sarah Blee
Client: London Borough of Camden, Heritage Lottery Fund, Friends of Alexandra Road Park

Alexandra Road Park is at the heart of the large Alexandra and Ainsworth social housing estates, which were designed in 1968 by architect Neave Brown.

The park has been fully restored with £1.5 million from the Heritage Lottery Fund's Parks for People program, which is jointly funded by the Big Lottery Fund. The refurbished space preserves the sense of wilderness of the original Modernist park while opening views and incorporating new play features designed by Erect Architecture.

Landscape architect Janet Jack worked in conjunction with Brown to design the green space within the estate. Completed in 1979, Jack used strategic planting design to transform the narrow and windy site into a series of sheltered spaces.

The 4.2-acre (1.7-hectare) linear park was structured by diagonal paths that created a series of outdoor rooms, and each had a different character and originally incorporated playgrounds also designed by Jack. A dramatic three-dimensional landscape of ridges and valleys surrounded the park, offering excellent views from raised gardens and plazas, as well as more intimate sunken spaces.

The park proved to be an early exemplar of wholly integrated sustainable urban drainage design, as it utilized the contours of the site to create a network of land drains and gravel infiltration trenches that enabled water to be slowly released into the underlying substrata.

Alexandra Road Park fell into disrepair over time and all play equipment was eventually removed. In 2010 a group of local residents formed a partnership with Camden Council and compiled a submission for funding to repair and improve the park. In 2013 the project received £1.5 million in funding through the Parks for People program.

Engagement with residents of all ages, as well as with Janet Jack, informed the design process led by landscape architects J & L Gibbons.

They undertook work to improve and rejuvenate the park while still enabling the original design intent to be experienced and appreciated by residents and visitors. This included restoring and enhancing the original park landscapes and planting; restoring the hard landscaping and improving accessibility; and improving biodiversity across the site.

The restoration of Alexandra Road Park was fascinating from the outset, involving the restoration of one of the most modern heritage assets that Heritage Lottery Fund have funded and cited as "the

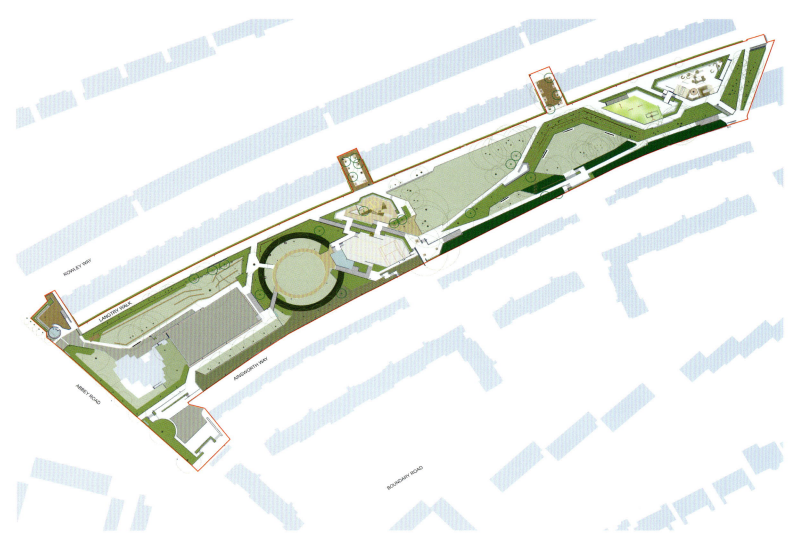

Alexandra Road Park landscape plan and materials

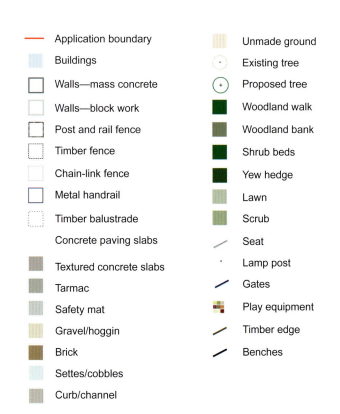

	Application boundary		Unmade ground
	Buildings		Existing tree
	Walls—mass concrete		Proposed tree
	Walls—block work		Woodland walk
	Post and rail fence		Woodland bank
	Timber fence		Shrub beds
	Chain-link fence		Yew hedge
	Metal handrail		Lawn
	Timber balustrade		Scrub
	Concrete paving slabs		Seat
	Textured concrete slabs		Lamp post
	Tarmac		Gates
	Safety mat		Play equipment
	Gravel/hoggin		Timber edge
	Brick		Benches
	Settes/cobbles		
	Curb/channel		

most significant landscape of its type in the UK." Many will be familiar with the iconic architecture of the estate designed by Neave Brown, but may not even know of the park designed by Janet Jack in 1979 which lies at the centre of the estate.

Erect Architecture designed four new play spaces for the site. These referenced and reinterpreted Jack's historic play features, while considering current best practice to reflect modern play theory.

1 Restored meadow and new planting
2 Lime trees with new underplanting

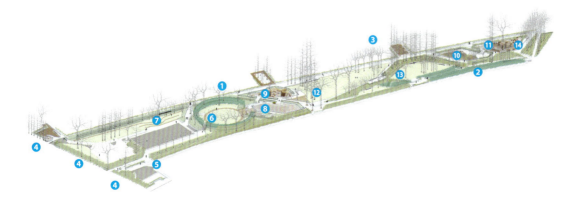

Character areas

1. Langtry Walk
2. Woodland Walk
3. Space between B Blocks
4. Seating areas near Abbey Road
5. Footbal pitch environs
6. Bowl
7. Playground 1 side park
8. Playground 2
9. Playground 3
10. Playground 4
11. Playground 5
12. Meadow
13. Mourd
14. Seating areas near Tenants Hall

Oblique view of the park identifying the character areas

1 Coppiced shrubberies and new interplanting
2 Playground 5 with restored original swing in foreground
3 New planting on birch bank with restored wall in foreground
4 Woodland Walk
5 Bowl and newly-coppiced Yew hedge

1 Restored post and rail fencing alongside ramp and through birch bank
2 Restored walls of playground 3 with yellow play structure beyond
3 Playground 5 designed for younger children
4 View of Langtry Walk from Tenants Hall

Tongva Park

Location: Los Angeles, United States
Area: 7 acres (2.8 hectares)
Completion date: 2014
Landscape design: James Corner Field Operations
Photography: Tim Street-Porter, Joakim LIoyd Raboff, James Corner Field Operations
Client: City of Santa Monica

The Tongva Park development project has seen a former parking area in Santa Monica, Los Angeles, transformed into a dynamic topography and lush landscape of rolling hills, meadows, and gardens. It is now celebrated as an important destination and center for the community and has received numerous national design awards.

An extensive community process shaped the design, which took inspiration from the Southern California arroyo landscape. The layout of the park is divided into four sections: Garden Hill has a series of seating alcoves and intimate display gardens that showcase Southern California plants; Discovery Hill is a play space for children with hill slides, a music wall, water play, and other custom play structures embedded in the lush and shaded landscape; Observation Hill offers views of the ocean and neighboring vicinity; and Gathering Hill provides a large multipurpose lawn.

Tongva Park's water elements aid sustainability and make use of biological filtration and closed potable water systems. Planted areas are irrigated with water from the nearby Santa Monica Urban Runoff Recycling Facility (SMURRF). Irrigated water and stormwater are maintained on site through the natural movement of water into bioswales at the base of almost every hill in the park.

Due to these design elements, daily water consumption for the irrigated park landscape and the water features is less than the average level of the city.

The sustainability of the green space is not only measured in terms of ecology, water, energy, and materials, but also in terms of social vibrancy. Walking trails and loops, bicycle parking areas, and inclusive play spaces for all ages and abilities function as places that promote the health and well-being of the people who experience them.

1 At 18-feet (5.5-meters) high, Observation Hill offers views of the ocean and pier. It buffers noise from Ocean Avenue and quietens the park interior
2 The green space is modeled on healthy native environments, and interconnected botanical, hydrologic, and topographic systems work to provide a restored ecosystem
3 Details of the flowerbed
4 Water Bay at the entrance to Tongva Park

Site plan

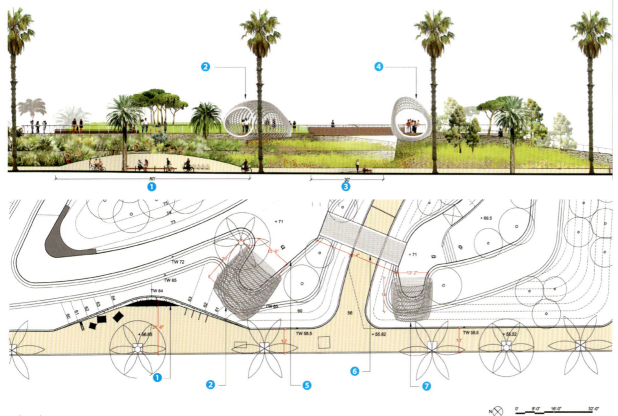

Elevation 1

① Bike bay
② Pier overlook
③ Entry
④ Ocean overlook
⑤ Continuous wood railing
⑥ Glulam footbridge
⑦ Ocean overlook

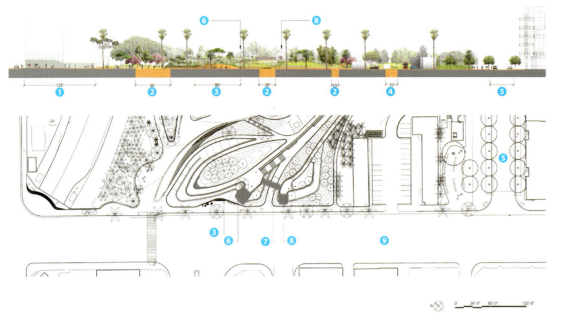

① Green screen
② Entry
③ Bike bay
④ Service entry
⑤ Olympic Drive
⑥ Pier overlook
⑦ Glulam footbridge
⑧ Ocean overlook
⑨ Ocean Avenue

Elevation 2

1 Rolling topography at Garden Hill provides an ideal surface for grasses, succulents, aloes, agaves, and seasonal bulbs
2 Small garden with lush vegetation
3 Observation Hill
4 Water play area with boulders at Discovery Hill is popular with children
5 Overlooks at Observation Hill are fabricated from plasma-cut plate steel

Philips Ridge Park

Location: Richmond Hill, Canada
Area: 7.91 acres (3.2 hectares)
Completion date: 2015
Landscape design: Schollen & Company Inc.
Photography: Mark Schollen
Client: Town of Richmond Hill

Philips Ridge Park is located on the Oak Ridges Moraine in Richmond Hill, Toronto. The plan and design of the green space interprets the physiography of the area, including the stratification of soils, undulating topography, and presence of underlying aquifers that serve as the water supply to both Lake Ontario and Lake Simcoe. The green space is located near a residential area and has become one of the most important places for residents to hold leisure activities. It has a playground and rock-climbing wall for children, as well as a sports court and hill slide.

The landscape design includes a wetland, wildflower meadow, woodland and grassland. The focal point is a 295-feet (90-meter) long wall that forms the base of a kame-like landform. The façade of the wall, designed in collaboration with artist Stephen Cruise, is reminiscent of a vertical slice through the Moraine landform, exposing the layers of sand, silt, and stone that characterize the formation.

The design incorporates a number of Low Impact Development initiatives including enhanced swales and a polishing wetland to manage stormwater runoff, permeable pavement to reduce the extent of impervious area, and plantings comprising native indigenous species.

Concept plan

1. Boulevard trees
2. Existing catchbasin with modification for new drainage inlet
3. Bench and trash receptacle
4. Concrete wall at back of basketball hoop
5. Ornamental metal fence at wall top exposed wall correspond with berm topography
6. Asphalt walkway 7.9-ft (2.4-m) wide, light duty
7. Soccer goal nets and posts
8. Soccer field
9. Existing fence
10. Woodland
11. Sport court
12. Junior soccer pitch
13. Asphalt walkway
14. Unit paving
15. Armourstone edge
16. Causeway/swale edge with armourstone
17. Post and paddle wood fence
18. Existing sidewalk/link to Town sidewalk
19. Trash receptacle
20. Post and paddle wood fence
21. Permeable paving with subdrain
22. Wetland
23. Boulevard trees
24. "Moraine" landform
25. Safety surface at base of wall
26. Senior play area
27. Shade structure
28. Meadow

Overall conceptual master plan

1 Feature wall with moraine stratigraphy and rock-climbing hand-holds
2 Feature wall with interpretive inlays
3 Playground with hill slide

Section drawing

① Buffer to facilities/property line
② Play-out line
③ Junior soccer field
④ Existing grade line
⑤ Proposed grade line
⑥ Moraine landform
⑦ Seating area
⑧ Interpretive wall
⑨ Paved area
⑩ Wetland
⑪ Ornamental fence
⑫ Proposed interpretive wall/traversing wall
⑬ Sidewalk planting
⑭ Street line
⑮ Proposed wetland
⑯ Sidewalk
⑰ Milos Road

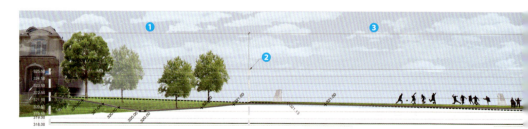

Cross-section through moraine landform

Elevation of feature wall

1 Trail to crest of Moraine landform
2 Landform-themed sports court
3 Feature rock at viewpoint on Moraine landform
4 Watercourse crossing detail
5 Meadow landscape at pavilion

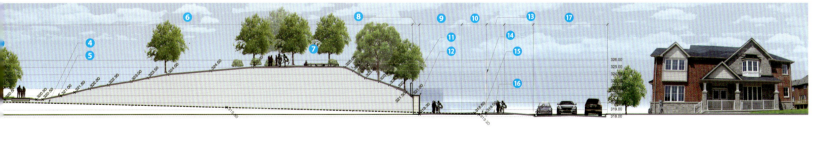

Lan Kila Pat Khlong Jan

Location: Bangkok, Thailand
Area: 2.77 acres (1.12 hectares)
Completion date: 2015
Landscape design: Shma Company Limited
Photography: Jirasak Thongyuak
Client: Lan Kila Pat, Klong Jan Community Housing, Office of H.M. Principal Private Secretary, Thai Health Promotion Foundation (ThaiHealth)

Lan Kila Pat is a neighborhood park in Bangkok, and his Majesty the King initiated the project for the low-income housing community that surrounds the site. The development transformed an abandoned park into a green space providing a wide range of sport and recreational facilities that can contribute to a healthy lifestyle for all users.

Landscape architects Shma collaborated with Arsom Silp Institute of the Arts to undertake a public participation program that enabled local residents to express and exchange ideas and suggestions. The designers compiled a wish list and problem list that helped them to understand the actual needs of various groups in the community and to plan appropriate spaces and activities at the right locations. The inclusive approach not only resulted in a successful physical design, but also gives the community a sense of belonging, which will contribute to a stronger society.

The design concept took the theme "Charn Baan"—the terrace of a traditional Thai house—because the green space is located by a canal. The theme can be seen in the modern interpretation of the distinctive benches with backrest details.

Designers used local and affordable materials and maintained all existing trees. The green space also features varied species of fragrant flowering trees in the senior activity area and edible trees to provide a natural habitat for birds and other wildlife species. The large lawn improves the local climate and purifies and stores rainwater.

1 Artificial wood and native plants create a peaceful atmosphere along the walkway
2 Boxing equipment for children and adults
3 Bird House helps retain existing natural ecology

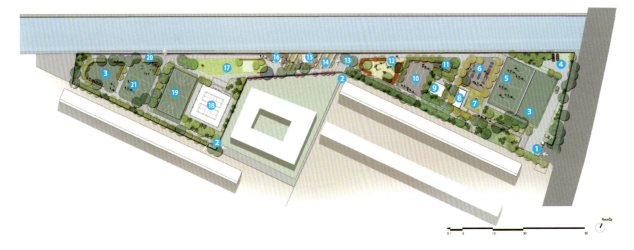

① Main entrance
② Sub entrance
③ Multipurpose lawn
④ Car park
⑤ Football field
⑥ Senior activity area
⑦ Sculpture garden
⑧ Exhibition honoring His Majesty, the King
⑨ Washroom
⑩ Chess game area
⑪ Petanque area
⑫ Children's playground
⑬ Children's play area
⑭ Herb garden
⑮ Cat house
⑯ Canal pavilion
⑰ Thai sport lawn
⑱ Indoor badminton area
⑲ Basketball fitness station
⑳ Outdoor fitness station
㉑ Sepak takraw field

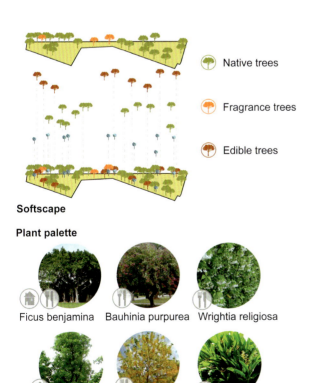

Softscape

Plant palette

Ficus benjamina

Bauhinia purpurea

Wrightia religiosa

Dolichandrone serrulata

Cassia fistula

Heliconia

Native trees

Fragrance trees

Edible trees

1 "Charn Baan" benches are designed to be adaptable for various
   needs, uses, and purposes
2 Playground offers a fun and tactile learning environment for children
   to develop physical and cognitive skills

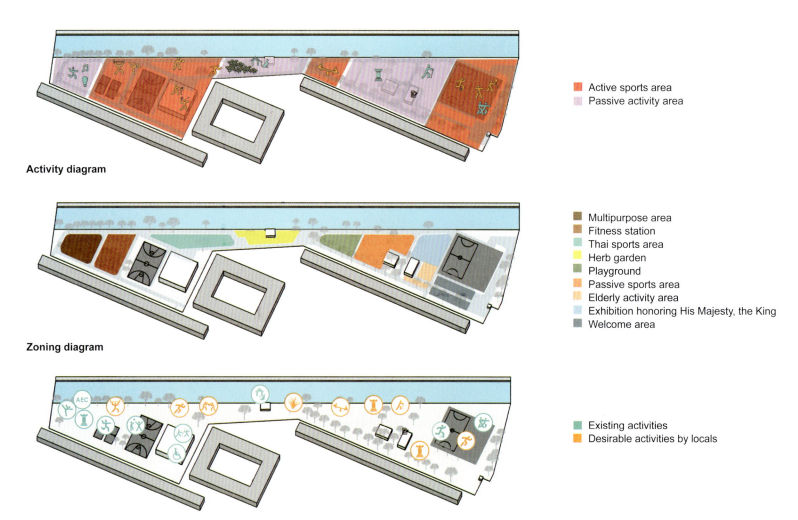

Activity diagram

- 🟧 Active sports area
- 🟪 Passive activity area

Zoning diagram

- 🟫 Multipurpose area
- 🟫 Fitness station
- 🟩 Thai sports area
- 🟨 Herb garden
- 🟩 Playground
- 🟧 Passive sports area
- 🟧 Elderly activity area
- 🟦 Exhibition honoring His Majesty, the King
- ⬜ Welcome area

Locals' desirable activity diagram

- 🟩 Existing activities
- 🟧 Desirable activities by locals

3 Outdoor gymnasium provides fitness equipment for community members
4 Children play games inside the enclosed "Charn Baan" seating area
5 Community members actively participate in cultivating Thai herbs in the herb garden

Bürgerpark Paunsdorf

Location: Leipzig, Germany
Area: 32 acres (13 hectares)
Completion date: 2014
Landscape design: häfner jiménez betcke jarosch landschaftsarchitektur gmbh
Photography: Hanns Joosten, Jens Betcke, Thomas Jarosch
Client: The City of Leipzig

Designed in the 1980s, Heiterblick is a housing estate situated in the north of Leipzig, with the new Porsche and BMW manufacturing plants and Leipzig-Dresden motorway close by. The City of Leipzig undertook an initiative to offer local residents a place to engage in recreation and be close to nature, as well as providing a protected living space for endangered wildlife. The project saw the development of Bürgerpark Paunsdorf; once a no-man's land on the periphery of the housing estate it is now part of Leipzig's largest outdoor development.

A circulation ring forms the core of the landscape, passing through the housing estate and recalling the ring road around the center of Leipzig. It also forms a boundary between the dense urban development and open landscape, giving order to public space and directing orientation. The pathway offers elevated viewpoints at each of the six bends, marked by blocks of trees. The recreation area has meeting and resting points, playgrounds, sports grounds, sites for sledding, mountain biking, and many other activities, and it surrounds a new lake, which also works as a rainwater retention reservoir.

The old Heiterblick barracks, formerly used for military training, create a highly valuable area of ecological interest. Indigenous herds of cattle cultivate the landscape and maintain the open space. Przewalski horses also enhance the experience and a path around the pasture is designed to protect the fauna.

1 Bürgerpark Paunsdorf is part of a 291-acre (118-hectare) long-term project
2 New water landscape in front of the Paunsdorf Nord district
3 Serene lake within the green space
4 Pathway near the lake leads to the surrounding residential area

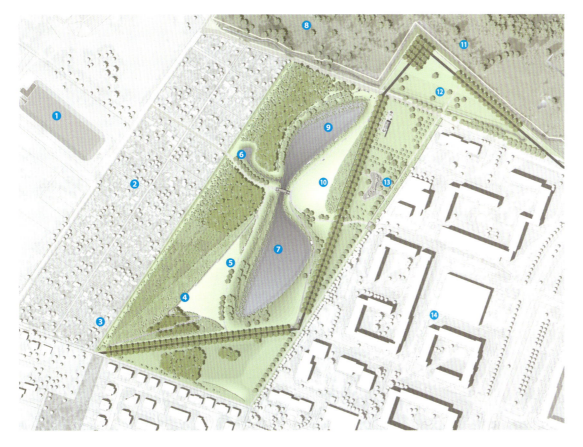

Site plan
1. Rain-storage reservoir
2. Allotment
3. Metaseqouia glyptostroboides
4. Hill, south, with plateau
5. Bürgerpark
6. Water input
7. Lake, south
8. Meadow (former military ground)
9. Lake, north
10. Hill, north
11. Metaseqouia glyptostroboides
12. Terrace Bürgerpark
13. Playground
14. Pausnsdorf Nord district
15. Circular walk lined with Quercus palustris trees

1 Water landscape
2-3 Impression of circular walk during different seasons

Plan of rainwater retention management

① Rainwater input
② Pressure-relief pipeline for stormwater input
③ Detail of overflow barrier
④ Stormwater-intake basin
⑤ Artificial lake for rainwater retention
⑥ Detail of pump system and emergency overflow

Maßstab 1 : 1000

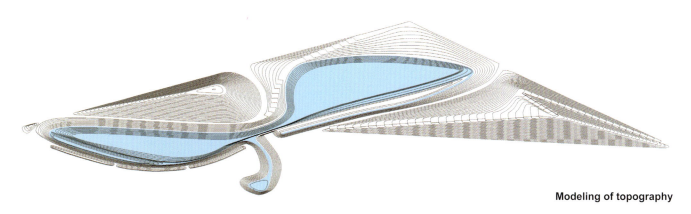

Modeling of topography

sØnæs Climate Park

Location: Viborg, Denmark
Area: 24.7 acres (10 hectares)
Completion date: 2015
Landscape design: Møller & Grønborg A/S
Photography: Helene Hoyer Mikkelsen, Carsten Ingemann, Viborg Municipality, Møller & Grønborg A/S
Client: Viborg Municipality, Energi Viborg Spildevand

sØnæs Climate Park is a large recreational green space situated close to the shoreline of Lake Søndersø near the center of Viborg, Denmark. While the area formerly hosted football fields, it was often useless due to being covered by water from the adjacent lake and its wet marshy soil.

The redevelopment project called for a park that could accommodate recreational activities for nearby residents of all ages, protect the hinterland against flooding, and respond to climate changes. sØnæs demonstrates how climate protection and sustainable urban drainage system-based solutions are capable of contributing to a recreational park and new aquatic environment. Thereby the project contains a triple function—by combining a recreational park, climate protection, and finally cleaning the water from the hinterland before it is released into the lake. Thus, the project illustrates how climate protection and recreational activities can be combined with water purification.

Danish company Møller & Grønborg designed the 24.7-acre (10-hectare) redevelopment, which maintains a natural character and supports increased biodiversity and stormwater management. The landscape is a multilevel and curved terrain with a meandering lake (with a volume capacity of 441,433 cubic feet [12,500 cubic meters]) that frames the area and creates an internal island—Ø meaning 'island' in Danish.

When rainstorms occur, the lake's water level rises and water is directed into internal basins on the island of sØnæs, which function as detention ponds, and thereby change the landscape to a system of dikes and lakes. Together the lake and basins on the island have a total capacity of 1,712,761 cubic feet (48,500 cubic meters). The aquatic environment maintains rainwater in the sØnæs area for 24 hours, during which time it is purified and the phosphorus discharge to Søndersø reduced by 60 percent.

The aquatic landscape is linked by a main path that has a variety of areas, such as beach, sun-facing staircase, reed forest, and landing/fishing bridge, along its length. Two pavilions on the path are for information and recreational purposes. Different play equipment is located in the internal area of the park and encourages children to play in wet areas where the water surface is constantly changing. The curved landscape maintains the natural character and further supports an overall natural improvement of the area with increased biodiversity and experience of nature.

sØnæs is realized through its close cooperation with the citizens of Viborg and the municipality. The project is selected as an illustration project supported by Vandplus, which is a collection of Realdania, Lokale- oganlægsfonden and Naturstyrelsen. The project will be exhibited at the La Biennale di Venezia (Venice Biennale) 2016.

1 sØnæs is a multilevel and curved terrain with a meandering lake and pathways
2 sØnæs is situated close to the shoreline of Lake Søndersø near the center of Viborg, Denmark

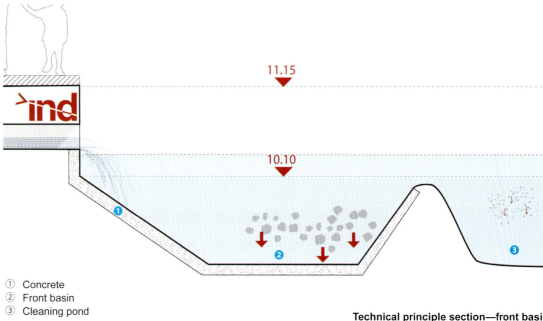

① Concrete
② Front basin
③ Cleaning pond

Technical principle section—front basin

Site plan

1. Boat jetty
2. Beach
3. Pumps
4. Sun-facing staircase
5. Meadow and marsh
6. Intake
7. Lake pavillion
8. Overflow
9. Lake
10. Island
11. Main path
12. Parking area
13. Information pavilion
14. Water-measuring sticks
15. Path

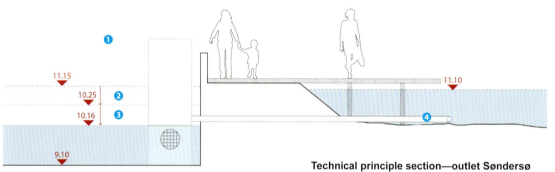

① sØnæs
② Pump 2 starts
③ Pump 1 starts
④ Outlet

Technical principle section—outlet Søndersø

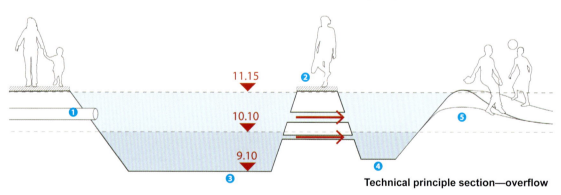

① Inlet
② Overflow from cleaning pond to stream
③ Cleaning pond
④ Stream
⑤ Island

Technical principle section—overflow

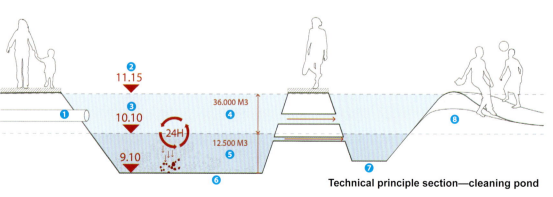

① Inlet
② Maximum capacity
③ Permanent water level
④ Variable volume
⑤ Permanent volume
⑥ Cleaning pond
⑦ Stream
⑧ Island

Technical principle section—cleaning pond

1 Concrete path crosses the lake and connects the island to the mainland
2 Stepping stones create a boundary around the front basin and offer an alternative path across the water
3 Red pavilion provides an area for various recreational activities
4 Varying water levels conceal and reveal stepping stones, increasing and decreasing the challenge of crossing the lake
5 Various activities encourage children to play

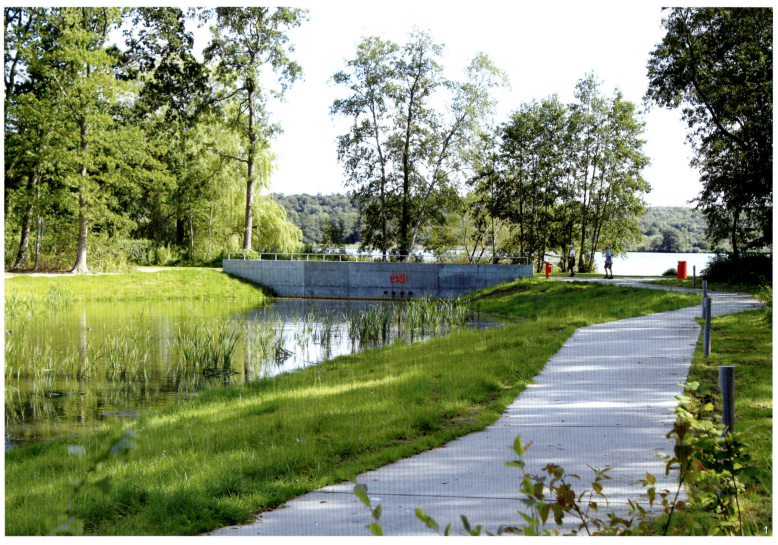

1 Accessible path connects sØnæs
2 Curved landscape supports the natural environment
3 Playing activities are closely related to the theme of water
4 sØnæs landscape can be used for various activities

① Cleaning pond
② Overflow
③ Basin 1
④ Basin 2
⑤ Basin 3
⑥ Basin 4

Technical principle section—detention ponds

Conversion Estienne-et-Foch Barrack

Location: Landau, Germany
Area: 66.7 acres (27 hectares)
Completion date: 2015
Landscape design: A24 Landschaft
Photography: Hanns Joosten
Client: LGS Landau 2015 GmbH

The center of the conversion area Estienne-et-Foch Barrack in Landau Germany is sizable neighborhood park, Germany, that incorporates the unique features of the Vorderpfalz region thereby forging a close relationship with its location. The planning and design of the green space successfully integrate nature conservation and recreational uses. A landscaped axis links the urban residential and leisure areas with the Ebenberg Nature Reserve bordering the grounds of the State Horticultural Show, and the observation tower at the end of the axis provides a view of the city and green space.

The development complements both the military barracks and new housing constructions, and a pool of water with lush vegetation lies at the heart of the green space. Its design is inspired by the tectonic upheaval characteristic of the Upper Rhine's rift valley. The recreation area is situated on the grounds of a former coal yard, and its structure makes use of the remains of unused railway facilities and their natural overgrowth of vegetation.

Stormwater is drained through the wide expansive lawn and the risk of waterlogging is prevented with underground packs of gravel, which are also at the playing fields on the campus. All paths are constructed with a slight incline so that rainwater drains through the lawn.

1　Wooden structures serve as seating
2　A ribbon of shrubs in the neighborhood park
3　Structural ramp to lookout platform combines accessibility and design

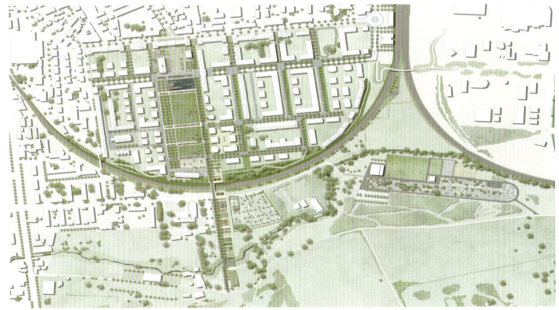

Overall plan

4 Skatepark with dirt-bike track in background
5 Sports center completes the new recreational
facility and attracts people from across Landau

Section of the landscape axis / section of the ramp

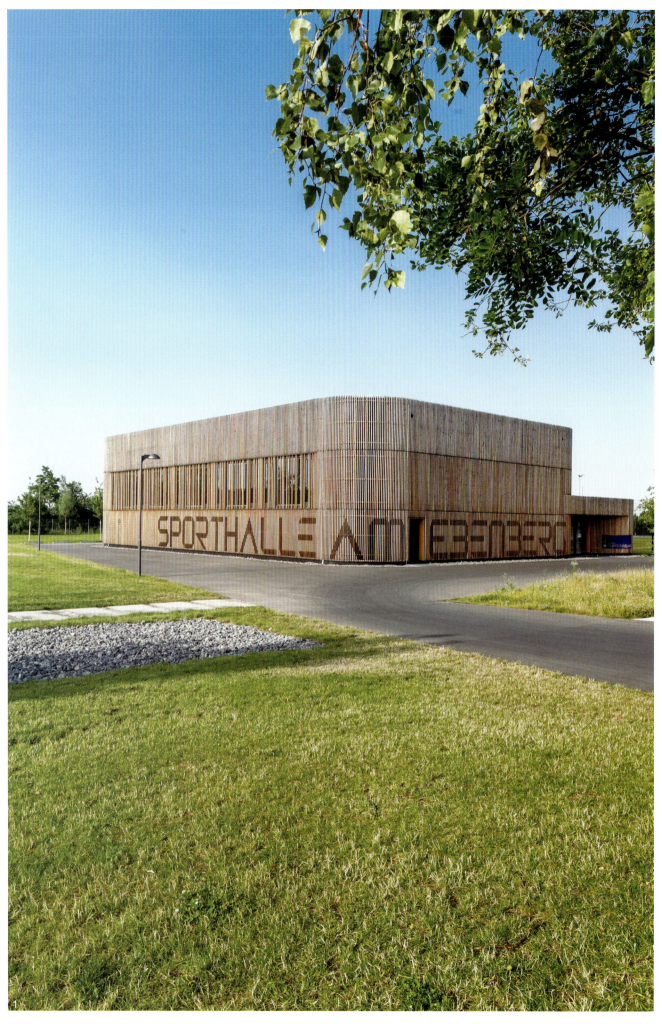

1 Sports center designed by Swillus Architekten
2 Slanted perimeter around the lawn reflects the tectonics of the region

Section—recreational facility

Section—neighborhood park

1 Benches by the sand court
2 Original ruderal vegetation has remained due to successive planting
3 Public access to Ebenberg Nature Reserve
4 Ruderal vegetation amongst wooden platform seating
5 The neighborhood park forms the center of the new residential quarter

Jincheng Botanical Garden (Children's Park)

Location: Shanxi, China
Area: 12.6 acres (5.1 hectares)
Completion date: 2011
Landscape design: Rehwaldt Landschaftsarchitekten
Photography: Rehwaldt Landschaftsarchitekten
Client: Greening Authority of Jincheng City, Shanxi Province

The redevelopment of Jincheng Botanical Garden (Children's Park) retained many of its characteristic features including valuable tree population, bonsai garden, and traditional bridge. It also maintained and extended the views into the green space and the visual connections between elements, which were established according to traditional Chinese gardens.

The redesign is based on a functional and conceptual gradation of space in a north-south direction forming three different zones. The southern part of the park has a modern, urban character and a contemporary entrance; the northern area represents tradition and hosts a historic bonsai garden and Muslim cemetery; the exhibition and event zone is located in the space in between. Park entrances have been added in the east and north to improve accessibility throughout the green space.

Landscape architects Rehwaldt took their inspiration from the park's surroundings: islands, boardwalks, lakes, and colorful and species-rich forests. The organic shapes of the agricultural landscape influenced the design of the exhibition area, and the plaza was derived from the city's urban structures.

To achieve the concept of the modern urban zone versus the traditional landscape zone, the trees have been placed in loose patterns in the south and dense groups in the north; the existing trees were integrated into the new design. Big shrubs, bamboo, and hedges were planted in the west and north in order to create private and visually protected areas, while hedges frame the eastern park edges. The large park meadow is used for recreation activities and the remaining lawn has multicolored and decorative planting.

The waterfront has been designed to look natural with gentle lake banks, shrubs, and traditional Chinese stones. It facilitates water access and children can experience the island and wetlands in the northeast of the lake via the boardwalk.

1 Lake and promenade
2 Swampland with boardwalks
3 Waterside along exhibition hall
4 Path in the northern park

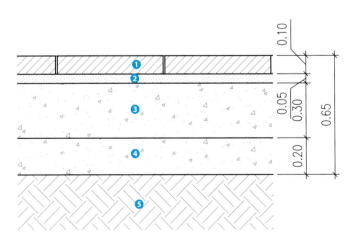

Plate covering

① Natural stone plate, 4 in (10 cm)
② Aggregate sand mixture, 2 in (5 cm)
③ Crushed stone base, 1 ft (30 cm)
④ Frost protection layer, 8 in (20 cm)
⑤ EV2 min. 6,527 psi (45 MN/m²)

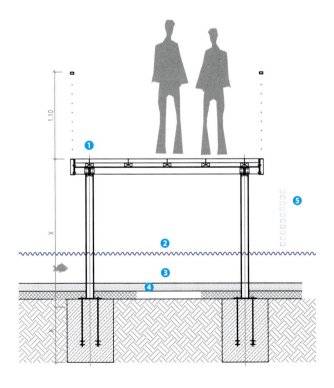

Longitudinal section Q1-Q1

① Horizontal stainless steel rope D: 0.2 in (4 mm)
② Water surface
③ Lake bed
④ Waterproof layer (eg: loam)
⑤ Total height depends on the height and water surface of site

156

Section

① Concrete foundation
② Concrete angle bracket
③ Purification layer of crushed stone 0/32
④ Bridge pier
⑤ Waterproof connector
⑥ Coated steel guardrail
⑦ Stainless steel rope in the middle of guardrail
⑧ Water fluctuation
⑨ Water surface
⑩ Lakebed
⑪ Waterproof layer (eg: loam)
⑫ Total height depends on the height and water surface of site

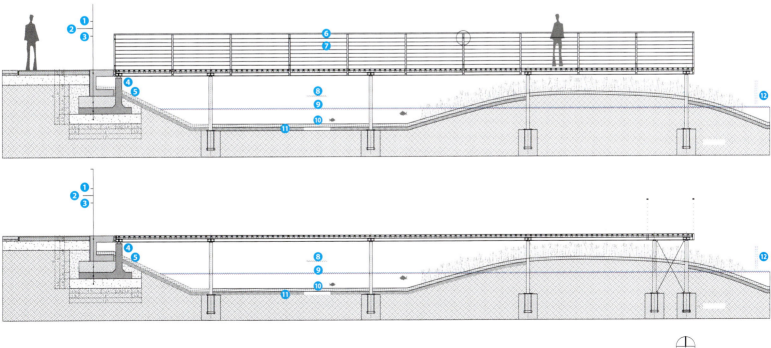

Detail—boardwalk

1:50

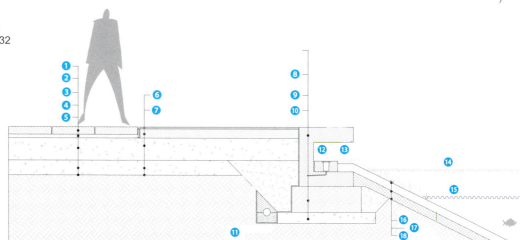

Paving plan

Cross-section

① Natural stone 4 in (10 cm), 40/60/10
② Mixture crushed stone and sand 2 in (5 cm), 0/32
③ Load-bearing layer crushed stone 1 ft (30 cm), 0/32
④ Frost-protection layer 8 in (20 cm), 0/45
⑤ Coefficient of compaction min. 45MN/m²
⑥ Frost-protection layer 8 in (20 cm), 0/45
⑦ Coefficient of compaction min. 45MN/m²
⑧ Concrete foundation
⑨ Purification layer of crushed stone 0/32
⑩ Coefficient of compaction min. 45MN/m²
⑪ Osmotic pipe
⑫ Reflector
⑬ Light zone
⑭ Water fluctuation
⑮ Water level
⑯ Lawn
⑰ Topsoil 4 in (10 cm)
⑱ Lake waterproof layer

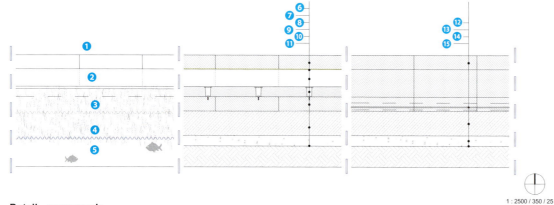

Detail—promenade

1 : 2500 / 350 / 25

Profile

① Lake-Promenade
② Light zone/concealed concave joint
③ Water fluctuation
④ Water surface
⑤ Lake
⑥ Reflector
⑦ Light zone/concealed concave joint
⑧ Recessed spotlight
⑨ Mortar bed
⑩ Load-bearing layer of crushed stone 0/32
⑪ Coefficient of compaction min. 45MN/m²
⑫ Lighting cable channel
⑬ Concrete foundation
⑭ Load-bearing layer of crushed stone 0/32
⑮ Coefficient of compaction min. 45MN/m²

1 Bamboo garden
2 Landscape sequence in the northern park
3-5 Plantings along the pathways
6 Plaza at park entrance

Muscota Marsh Park

Location: New York, United States
Area: 1.2 acres (0.5 hectares)
Completion date: 2013
Landscape design: James Corner Field Operations
Photography: James Corner Field Operations, Julienne Schaer
Client: Columbia University

Muscota Marsh Park is a 1.2-acre (0.49 hectare) public green space adjacent to Inwood Hill Park in Manhattan, New York City. It consists of a restored salt marsh; freshwater wetlands; and an open park area fitted with furnishing, lighting, planting, lawns, and decks. Muscota Marsh Park caters to a wide range of people and builds on the latent ecology of the site, aiming to enrich the biodiversity of the Harlem River Valley.

The design is inspired by the area's tidal flats and mudways, which attract an array of diverse species, many of which are rare in the region. The design targets wildlife that favor the close proximity of the salt marsh and the freshwater wetlands, including wading birds such as Great Blue Heron and Snowy Egret, and leopard frogs and ribbed mussels.

The diverse palette of native wetland plants provide an excellent habitat, as well as dramatic colors and textures, seasonal change, and an audible rustling of grasses. Freshwaters are organized as three-tier ponds that progressively receive, treat, and slow stormwater runoff before it enters the tidal system in order to improved water quality in the river.

Designed with soft materials, the park is 80 percent pervious and able to withstand periodic inundation. The electrical conduits are continuous with splicing occurring above at light fixtures heads.

1 Muscota Marsh Park is located east of the Harlem River Valley
2 Designed with soft materials, the park is 80 percent pervious and able to withstand periodic inundation

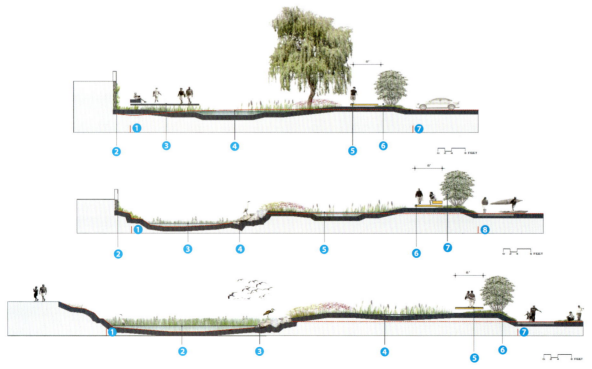

Typical sections

Section 1

① Property line
② Moss and fern wall
③ Marsh walk
④ Freshwater wetland
⑤ Deck promenade
⑥ Baccharis halimifolia hedge
⑦ Waterfront access area limit line

Section 2

① Property line
② Moss and fern wall
③ Spartina marsh
④ Stone bank
⑤ Freshwater wetland
⑥ Deck promenade
⑦ Baccharis halimifolia hedge
⑧ Waterfront access area limit line

Section 3

① Property line
② Spartina marsh
③ Stone bank
④ Freshwater wetland
⑤ Deck promenade
⑥ Baccharis halimifolia hedge
⑦ Waterfront access area limit line

Legend	
·—···—···—·	Property line
— — —	Project limit line
··········	3-ft (91-cm) high fence
⌒	Gate
—	Signage
	Wood decking
	Stone screenings
	Existing trees
	Proposed trees
	Lawn
	Upland planting TBD
	Freshwater wetland
	Salt marsh wetland
	Post light
	Asphalt
	Planting
	Existing permeable paver
	Trash receptacle
	Bench
	Picnic table

Site plan

① Guardrail
② Existing pier
③ Boulders
④ Existing riprap
⑤ Existing boat launch
⑥ Tidal mud flats
⑦ 3-ft (91-cm) high aluminum picket fence at project limit line
⑧ Crew shell house
⑨ Remmer boathouse
⑩ Baccharis halimifolia hedge
⑪ Custom bench
⑫ Security booth
⑬ Freshwater wetland
⑭ Weir
⑮ Salt marsh
⑯ ADA ramp
⑰ Picnic area
⑱ Swale
⑲ Inwood Hill Park
⑳ Bike racks
㉑ Entrance
㉒ Existing bollards
㉓ Existing boulders
㉔ Existing stone wall
㉕ Seating

1 Wood decking and walls
2 Seating for relaxation and wildlife observation
3 The design targets wildlife that prefer locations where saltwater marsh and freshwater marsh are in close proximity
4 The park provides the public with waterfront access
5 The open park area is fitted with furnishing, lighting, planting, lawns, and decks

Henry Palmisano Park

Location: Chicago, United States
Area: 27 acres (10.9 hectares)
Completion date: 2010
Landscape design: site design group, ltd.
Photography: site design group, ltd.
Client: Chicago Park District

Henry Palmisano Park is located in one of Chicago's residential and historic neighborhoods where it benefits community members and local commerce. The former quarry and landfill has been transformed into a green space for residents of Bridgeport, which is isolated from lake front amenities and historical parks by two major highways. At 27-acres (11-hectares) it increases the amount of green space in the area by 200 percent.

Henry Palmisano Park has spurred urban regeneration in various ways. Prior to construction, residents complained about thick layers of dust and unsightly barbed wire. Post-construction, the area has seen new infrastructure, sidewalks, and additional public parking; and small-scale residential infill developments have been established on all sides of the park including new senior housing directly across the street.

The green space provides several native ecosystems, including prairie plant communities, simulated wetlands, and a large two-acre pond, to encourage visitors to explore and discover natural processes. All stormwater is directed towards the pond and wetlands instead of city sewers, and park users are encouraged to walk amongst the native wetland plantings and engage with the water that flows through the tiered educational wetlands.

The industrial history of the site inspired the variety of trails, recycled timber boardwalks, paths and steps made from recycled sidewalk slabs, running tracks, and metal grating walkways. Nature trails wind up and down hills, through native plantings and wildlife habitats, up to raised walkways with aerial views of the pond and exposed quarry walls, and down to the water and fishing pier. Visitors can experience breathtaking views from the top of "Mount Bridgeport," constructed from materials displaced from the former use of the site.

1 Palmisano Park manages, stores, and infiltrates all stormwater falling on site

2 Captured stormwater is used as an educational tool through a recirculating water feature that describes the natural water cycle

3 The park allows for several unprogrammed recreational uses. Shown here is a martial arts class on top of one of the fishing piers

4 The educational story about the water cycle begins at the fountain, with a circular water feature made up of layers meant to look like stratified limestone

5 Despite the many ramps and massive elevation changes, the park is universally accessible from the lowest point at the fishing pier, all the way up to the top of the mound

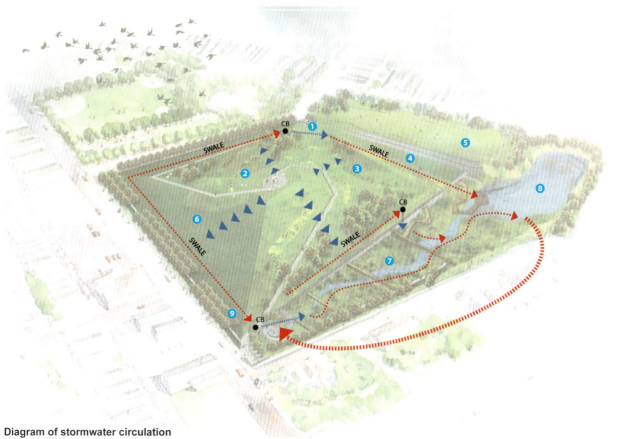

Diagram of stormwater circulation

① Plaza at southern entrance
② Boulder field
③ Prairie mound
④ Sloping lawn
⑤ Multipurpose field
⑥ Sledding hill
⑦ Wetlands
⑧ Fishing pond
⑨ Northeast main entry

1 Visitors are encouraged to interact with the natural features as way to educate them on the various plant and animal ecosystems found throughout the park

2 The numerous native ecosystems, plant communities, sustainable site elements, and recreational open space that make this park unique have also been the driving force that has made this a popular neighborhood and regional park for thousands of Chicagoland visitors

3 Rocky ground and lush green vegetation

4 During the 600-foot (183-meter) journey, the water splashes over recycled concrete and reclaimed limestone boulders found on the site during construction

5 Palmisano Park is a new kind of urban park that mixes industrial, educational, and ecological elements in a way that engages the user

Fairwater Park

Location: Western Sydney, Australia
Area: 23 acres (9.5 hectares)
Completion date: 2015
Landscape design: McGregor Coxall
Photography: McGregor Coxall, Simon Wood
Client: Frasers Property (formerly Australand)

Fairwater Park is the redevelopment of Ashlar Golf Course, formerly a residential housing development on a private site. Located in Blacktown, it is in close proximity to the Western Sydney CBD, and at the confluence of two large-scale engineered drainage systems. Vegetation on the site consists of a unique ecological system of retained endemic tree species.

Landscape architects McGregor Coxall took a holistic approach and collaborated with a number of specialized consultants. It developed a water-sensitive design response that de-engineers the drainage systems so they become a key component of the green space's new identity and open space network. The result is the establishment of two major water-based parklands, which are interconnected through an activated linear wetland environmental corridor that promotes wildlife.

Visitors to Fairwater Park can come into close contact with nature. Local flora has been retained and relocated to create a distinct and lush natural habitat, while tree-lined streetscapes lead to pockets of green. Shaded, family-friendly playgrounds provide meeting places and include children's play equipment made from natural materials.

The area has more than 3.7 acres (1.5 hectares) of ponds, wetlands, and waterways, and visitors can stroll along the boardwalk and view the water and wildlife from the bridge, while toddlers can enjoy the water play area.

As part of the flood planning process, McGregor Coxhall considered possible climate change impacts, including potential rainfall intensity increases. Based on this analysis, the site has been designed for the flood planning level (FPL) to include an additional 15 percent increase to allow for rainfall intensity.

- – - - – - - Site boundary
- STAGE 1 - Site boundary—stage 1
- —— Shared bike/pedestrian paths
- Stair
- Ramp

Walls and edges
- Pram crossing
- Dry stacked stone wall
- Concrete wall
- ====== Wall below
- Weir wall between upper and lower pond

Pavements
- Compacted decomposed granite
- Insitu concrete
- Timber decking with steel frame structure
- ○○○ Precast concrete steppers
- Precast concrete
- Bitumen (children's bike path with lane marking)
- GAL edge and gravel drainage strip
- Remnant sand bunkers
- Flush stone steppers
- Sandstone paved area with seat

Water elements
- Water body

Furniture + Fittings
- Seats
- Barbecue and bin enclosure
- Interactive art piece made from recycled site timber
- Sheltered seating
- Street lighting within the park

Planting
- Lawn
- Native grasses

Trees
- Existing tree retained
- Proposed native trees

Site plan
1. Upper lake
2. Lower lake
3. Fairway lawn
4. Triangle lawn
5. Grass terrace
6. Playground
7. Picnic area
8. Timber-deck boardwalk
9. Timber-deck bridge
10. Timber deck with no balustrade
11. Timber deck with balustrade on structure

1. Boardwalks offer visitors views and close access to the ponds, wetlands, and waterways
2. Drainage systems are a key component of the green space's identity and open space network

Section A—upper lake south deck

① Concrete path
② Hardwood timber deck on steel structure
③ Concrete edge wall
④ Security flat buffer zone
⑤ Upper lake

① Lot boundary
② Footing and stub for future boundary wall
③ Concrete path along future residential development
④ Proposed tree planting
⑤ Native grasses
⑥ Native grasses that withstand occasional inundation
⑦ Concrete edge wall
⑧ Security flat buffer zone
⑨ Upper pond
⑩ Security flat buffer zone
⑪ Curved dry-stone stack wall with top course fixed in place with hidden morter layer
⑫ GAL edge and gravel drainage strip
⑬ Compacted decomposed granite path
⑭ Concrete path along parklands
⑮ Large existing trees to be retained
⑯ Existing profile
⑰ Main boulevand

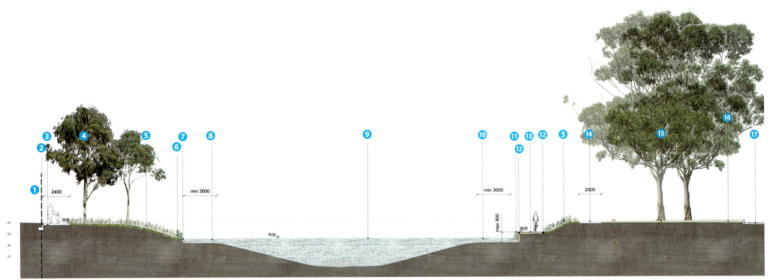

Section B—upper lake, cross-section through concrete path and curved stone wall

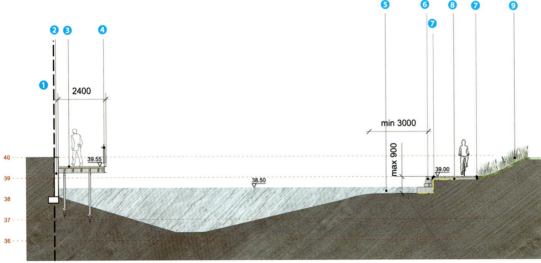

① Lot boundary
② Concrete wall
③ Hardwood timber boardwalk on steel structure and timber joists
④ Steel balustrade
⑤ Security flat buffer zone
⑥ Curved dry-stone stack wall with top course fixed in place with hidden morter layer
⑦ GAL edge and gravel drainage strip
⑧ Compacted decomposed granite path
⑨ Native grasses

Section C—upper lake, cross-section through timber boardwalk and curved stone wall

1 Local flora has been retained and relocated to create a distinct and lush natural habitat
2 The towering trees on the grass
3 Shaded areas provide meeting places for the community

1 Moss floating on the water looks very peaceful in the sun
2 Overlooking the park from the distance
3 Fairwater Park under the dark clouds
4 Visitors can stroll along the boardwalk and view the water and wildlife from the bridge

Section D—upper lake, cross-section through triangle lawn and curved stone wall

① Triangle lawn
② Large existing trees to be retained
③ Compacted decomposed granite path
④ Native grasses
⑤ Native grasses the can withstand occasional inundation
⑥ Concrete edge wall
⑦ Security flat buffer zone
⑧ Upper pond

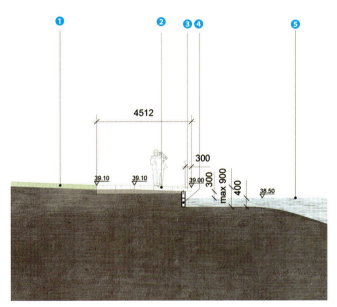

Section E—upper lake, precast concrete podium

① Grass area with concrete steppers
② Precast concrete units
③ Overhang to edge
④ Concrete edge wall
⑤ Upper pond

① Upper pond
② Precast concrete weir wall
③ Hardwood timber bridge on steel structure
④ Lower pond

Section F—weir wall and timber bridge

Parkstadt Schwabing

Location: Munich, Germany
Area: 99 acres (40 hectares)
Completion date: 2013
Landscape design: Rainer Schmidt Landscape Architects + City Planners
Photography: Raffaella Sirtoli, Michael Heinrich
Client: State Capital City Munich

Parkstadt Schwabing is a linear park in the north of Munich's inner city, and the twin Highlight Towers crown its southern end. Landscape architects Rainer Schmidt took Munich's aspect towards the Bavarian Alps as the concept for the green space and reflected the various alpine landscapes in its themed gardens. They are conceived as abstract representations of local landscape types and offer different atmospheres throughout the green space and during different seasons. These themed gardens recall mountain boulders, alpine lakes, meadows, and forest, while large lawns and native trees such as birches, pines, and oaks provide the experience of a continuous landscape.

Design guidelines have also been established for the vicinity. A planting guideline directs residents on how to arrange the green space in front of their house and front garden walls and paving stones have been custom designed to create a unique identity around the open space.

Sketch—rock garden　　　　　　　　　**Sketch—plan**

1 Garden with mountain
  boulders
2 Garden with gravel
3-4 Sand-filter system

1 Themed gardens with pavilion
2 Planted areas
3 Playground
4 Sports zones

Sketch—elevation plan

Sketch—grass mountains

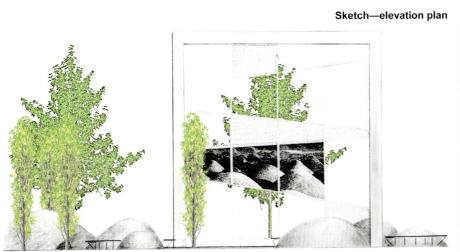

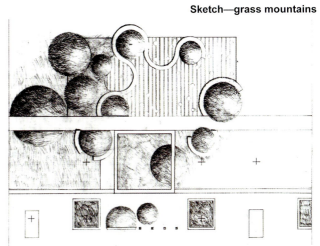

Water Collection Park "The Source" Zeist

Location: Zeist, Netherlands
Area: 5 acres (2 hectares)
Completion date: 2011
Landscape design: OKRA Landschapsarchitecten
Photography: Annie Beugel
Client: Vitens, municipality Zeist en Housing Corporation De Kombinatie

There are many groundwater collection areas throughout the Netherlands. While most are located in the open countryside outside of the cities, Zeist has expanded to such a point that a collection area is now located within the municipality. Water company Vitens and housing corporation de Kombinatie, in partnership with the local council, undertook an initiative to upgrade the former dog-walking area to a recreational green space for neighborhood residents.

The heavily-vegetated park is located in a forest clearing and its various components take advantage of the contrast between open and closed spaces. Playing fields are located in the open meadow; a woodland area is on the western edge and its forest atmosphere makes it an attractive place for exercise and play.

Water also has a prominent place with a water playground for children and pumping equipment from Vitens. A cartridge in the pathways is designed to filter water in the soil.

1 Football field adjacent to the woods
2 Pathway with benches
3 Chidren's playground
4 Existing trees surround the open space
   and function as windbreaks; some new
   tree groups added
5 Visualization of green space

Site plan

Schema

Windbreak trees

Grassland

Three open spaces

Woods around spaces

Route map

Activity area

1 Pathways circulate through the green space
2 Open space with mowed grass, rugged grass, and a meadow of natural flowers
3 Main pathway
4 Children's playground between the woods and pathway

Grorudparken

Location: Oslo, Norway
Area: 4.7 acres (1.9 hectares)
Completion date: 2013
Landscape design: LINK Arkitektur
Photography: Tomasz Majewski, Mads Erling Amundsen, Hundven-Clements Photography
Client: Oslo Water and Sewerage Works

Grorudparken is one of four new neighborhood parks in Groruddalen, Oslo. The development establishes a continuous landscape and recreation corridor from Lillomarka via Grorudparken through Leirfossen and Hølakøkka, and the design and construction process required significant cooperation between the city district and various municipal offices. The green space provides facilities for athletics, play, recreation, youth programs, social interaction, and cultural activities for a diverse local population.

The Alna River forms the central element of the layout, which integrates existing cultural and historical artifacts with new landscape experiences while also facilitating greater visual and physical access to the river itself. Outdoor lighting aids accessibility and population safety, and a site-specific lighting concept fosters an exciting spatial dimension and identity for the park.

Flood mitigation, stormwater management, and cleansing polluted subsurface materials proved both critical and technically challenging. However, significant improvements in water quality were achieved through various soil cleansing techniques. This includes stormwater from the surrounding areas being cleaned within bioremediation ponds before being released into the Alna River and Groruddammen, and a Norwegian pilot project that used phytoremediation and reduced carbon emissions associated with transporting soil for off-site remediation.

1 Center of park with Groruddamen pond
2 Tranquil environment of Groruddamen pond

Overall plan

3 Pathways providing access to and around Groruddamen pond
4 Groruddamen pond surrounded by trees

Central area dam and lake

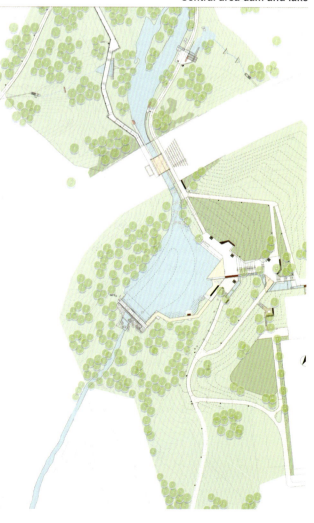

1 Children can play on the landscape around the dam
2 Groruddammen pond with jetty
3 Stairway is a part of the water purification scheme

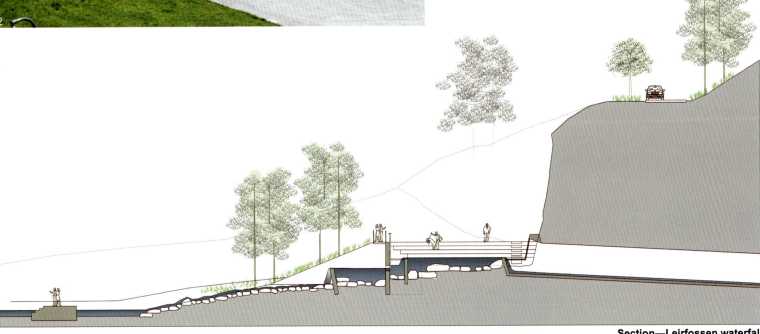

Section—Leirfossen waterfall

4 Groruddamen pond at the outlet of Alna River
5 Pathway alongside the pond

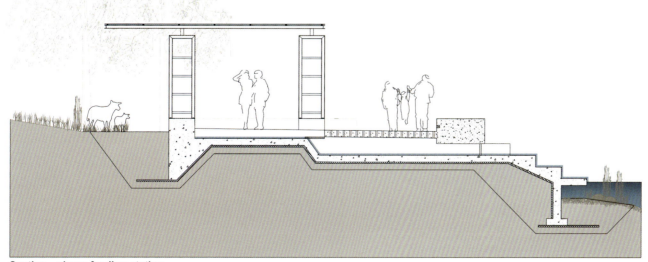

Section—sheep-feeding station

Catharina Amalia Park

Location: Apeldoorn, Netherlands
Area: 6.2 acres (2.5 hectares)
Completion date: 2014
Landscape design: OKRA Landschapsarchitecten
Photography: Annie Beugel
Client: Municipality of Apeldoorn

Now named for the Dutch princess, Catharina Amalia Park was formerly known as Brink Park. However, Brink Park was not a park in the recreational sense of the word; rather it was a parking area for cars and buses. Despite its appearance, the space had the potential to be transformed into an attractive green entrance to Apeldoorn and a recreational space for city residents. The end result combines underground parking, green space, and water, and is an example of how an urban area can be transformed from negative space to meaningful place.

Landscape architects OKRA designed an underground car park and aboveground park and created a plan to maximize green space and minimize infrastructure. The urban green space evokes an artificial image of the Veluwe streams with carved channels of water running longitudinally through the park. Different facilities and rest stops are positioned alongside the undulating landscape.

Site plan

Section

① Primary path
② Plantation
③ Footbridge
④ Waterway
⑤ Stream valley
⑥ Grass slope

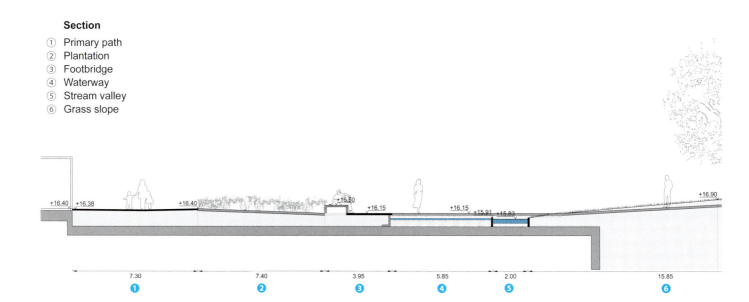

+16.40 +16.38   +16.40   +16.60   +16.15   +16.15 +15.91 +15.83   +16.90

7.30   7.40   3.95   5.85   2.00   15.85

① ② ③ ④ ⑤ ⑥

1 Grassland, garden, and buildings on both sides of the brook
2 Brook and grassland in front of the buildings
3 View of the park

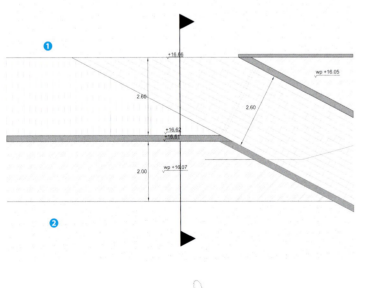

Detail 1 Scale: 1:50

① Conservative and protected concrete band
② About basin
③ Slope
④ Primary path
⑤ Stream valley

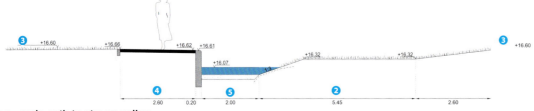

Section—main path to stream valley

1 Pathway besides the brook
2 Brook bed
3 Small bridge over brook
4 Main pathway through the green sapce
5 Pathway across the brook
6 Bridge across brook

Section—parking area

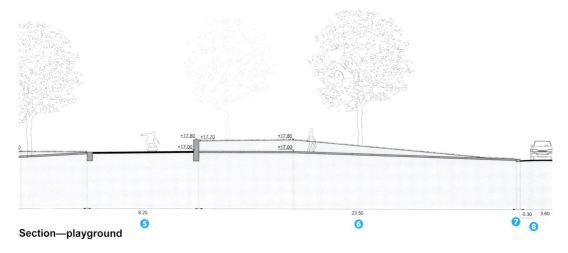

Section—playground

① Pavement
② Brinklaan Roadway
③ Parking area
④ Grassland
⑤ Skating
⑥ Grass slope/pathway
⑦ Roadway
⑧ Prince Willem Alexander Road

1 Planting adjacent to pathway
2 Trees, flowers, and grassland on both sides of pathway
3 Permeable paved pathway

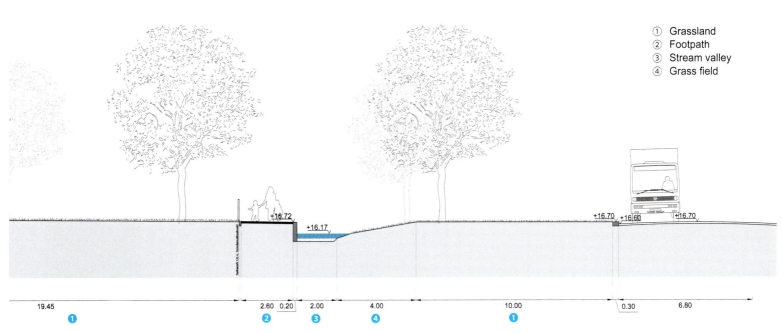

① Grassland
② Footpath
③ Stream valley
④ Grass field

Section—near Prince Willem Alexander Road

1 Benches alongside the stream
2 Water channel carved through the park
3 Pathways divide Catharina Amalia Park
  into various green spaces

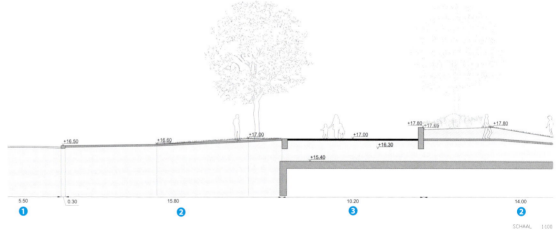

Section

① Green lane
② Grass slope/footpath
③ Grass slope
④ Path
⑤ Main path
⑥ Plantation
⑦ Footbridge/seating bench
⑧ Water plateau
⑨ Waterway
⑩ Grass slope

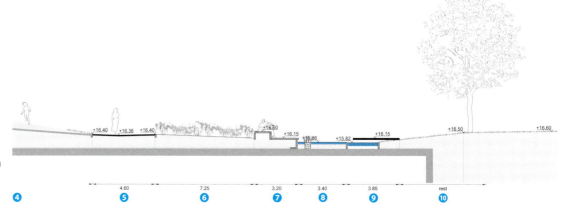

1 Recreational area is integrated into the landscape
2 Recreational area with unique color design
3 Trees and flowers on the grass slope
4 Landscape at the end of the pathway

Catene's Public Park in Marghera

Location: Marghera, Italy
Area: 19.8 acres (8 hectares)
Completion date: 2012
Landscape design: CZstudio associati , Paolo Ceccon Laura Zampieri architetti
Photography: CZstudio associati
Client: Municipality of Venice

Catene's Public Park in the Venetian hinterland redefines a fragment of land, which is surrounded by residential housing. The area has low-quality buildings and large territorial infrastructure as well as a lack of services and open public space. The park now serves as a meeting point for all members of the community, and town officials and local associations organize cultural and educational activities to teach visitors about the values of landscape and history.

The land is characterized by its distinctive agricultural topography and north-south system of drains and channels. The project preserved the existing trees and water structures, highlighting the importance of protecting, enhancing, and improving the area's agricultural and natural resources, while also conveying evidence of its cultural identity.

The project saw the construction of a lamination basin south of the park. It also reused soil from nearby excavation works as well as implementing other sustainable methods to maximize permeability of the soil and control the quantity and location of impermeable areas. The preserved wetlands are a rare example of an urban ecotone that can increase the environmental value of the local hydraulic system. In addition, storm water collection for irrigation contributes to the reduction of freshwater consumption.

Main pedestrian and vehicular paths are made of fiber-reinforced concrete and stabilized earth; secondary paths are graveled and follow the pre-existent agricultural channels to serve as an integral part of the underground drainage system. A concrete platform with two soccer fields and a basketball court on a synthetic surface leads to a panoramic terrace. Community buildings are made of exposed concrete, which is strongly related to the structure of the green space.

1 Lighting along the pathway in the sports area
2 Bird's-eye view
3 Meadowland near stabilized-earth pathways

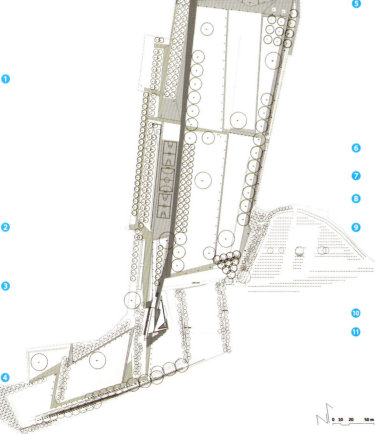

Site plan

① West entrance from Catene's plaza
② West entrance
③ 3,616 ft² (336 m²)
④ South entrance
⑤ North entrance
⑥ 4,660 ft² (433 m²)
⑦ 4,520 ft² (420 m²)
⑧ 4,660 ft² (433 m²)
⑨ Lamination basin
⑩ Wetlands
⑪ 1,076 ft² (100 m²)

0 10 20   50 m

1 Plantings of Celtis australis trees
2 Existing agricultural hydraulic system near the pavilion restaurant
3 View of the wetlands in summer (inaccessible to the public)
4 Path and sitting area south near wetlands in late summer
5 Gravel and stabilized-earth pathways

Section

① Wall-bench in reinforced concrete
② Fiber-reinforced concrete paving
③ Celtis australis
④ Gabion wall filled with limestone
⑤ Gravel path
⑥ Quercus rubra

Hydraulic system

- ◉ Wetland
- ● Reused agricultural ditches
- ○ Water pipelines
- ⋅ Gravel paths/microperforated pipes

Ground cover vegetaion

- Low grassland
- High grassland
- Wetland
- Wild grassland

Paths and surfaces

- Pedestrian concrete
- Vehicles concrete
- Gravel paths
- Stabilized-earth paths
- Synthetic surface
  (basketball court, soccer fields, bowls pitches)

San Serafino Public Park

Location: Verona, Italy
Area: 2.6 acres (1.1 hectares)
Completion date: 2010
Landscape design: Insitu Landscape Design Ltd.
Photography: Luca Baroni
Client: City of Oppeano

Oppeano is on an alluvial plain in Verona, northern Italy, and the typical landscape features ancient dried riverbeds, natural springs, and artificial rice fields. San Serafino Public Park is inspired by these different landscape features, which are connected by ramps and steps and used to define spaces, levels, and functions.

Structurally and functionally, the green space connects two major urban areas of Oppeano and importance is given to the central tree-lined and wooden-paved continuous path that crosses the park. It connects all the elements of the project including the parking area, square and fountain, pond, playground, and lawn. The stone-paved square is slightly recessed and forms an area where secondary paths merge; the fountain recalls the importance of water in the local landscape; and stone benches allow park users to sit and interact.

A bicycle path is part of an urban and regional cycling network crossing east-west through the park. A series of gardens parallel to the bicycle path accommodate a sequence of play areas, modulated with slight variations in height to define the areas for children of different ages. A nature educational area is at the northern border of the park and it is inspired by the local landscape, of which the central element is an artificial lake with a variety of aquatic vegetation.

Natural and man-made practices control flooding and form important elements of the local landscape. This includes grass swales that drain the water from the parking area and lawn; and a pond, which is connected to the existing Piganzolo Stream by a pump that catches infiltration water and ditch water.

1 Playground
2 View across the lawn to the square

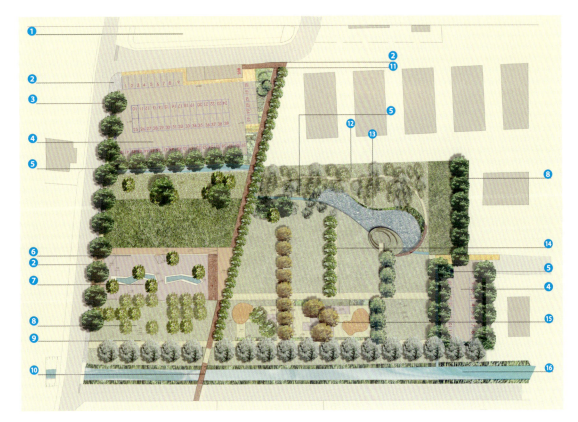

Overall plan

1. School
2. Pedestrian entrance
3. Tree row
4. Parking
5. Ditch
6. Square
7. Fountain
8. Lawn
9. Bike path
10. Footbridge
11. Main path
12. Wood
13. Little lake
14. Paths
15. Playgrounds
16. Piganzolo Stream

Flooring plan

① Bus stop
② Parking
③ Lessinia stone pavement
④ Gravel-look architectural concrete pavement
⑤ Deck pavement
⑥ Calcestre stabilized unpaved path
⑦ Lawn

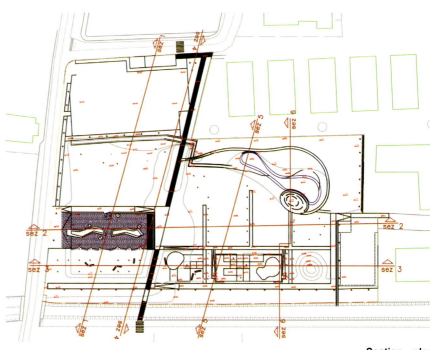

Section—plan

1 Children's play area
2 Lake and gabion wall
3 Bike path and playground
4 Square
5 Main path

Section 1

① Street work
② Piganzolo Stream
③ Bike path
④ Garden of the Senses
⑤ Square
⑥ Lawn
⑦ Ditch
⑧ Parking
⑨ Aldo Moro Street

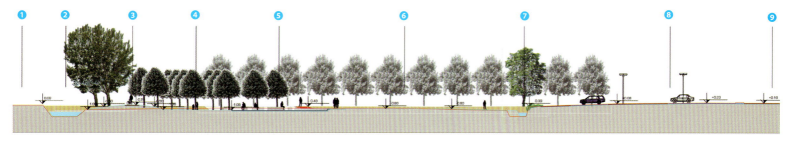

1 Square, lawn, and benches
2 Stream, footbridge, and bike path

Section 2

① Street
② Fountain
③ Square
④ Lighting pole
⑤ Pedestrain path
⑥ Path
⑦ Bike path
⑧ Ditch
⑨ East entrance
⑩ IV Route in November

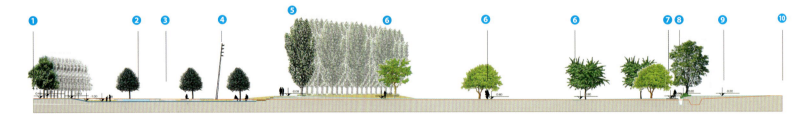

Section 3

① Garden of the Senses
② Playground
③ Hill
④ Parking

Section 4

① Aldo Moro Street
② Flowerbed parking
③ Parking area
④ Channel
⑤ Area devoted to multipurpose space
⑥ Square
⑦ Garden of the Senses
⑧ Bike path
⑨ Buffer zone
⑩ Drain
⑪ Street work

Section 5

① Street work
② Piganzolo Stream
③ Bike path
④ Playground
⑤ Lawn
⑥ Aldo Moro Street

Section 6

① Street work
② Piganzolo Stream
③ Bike path
④ Playground
⑤ Lake
⑥ Aldo Moro Street

Joel Weeks Park

Location: Toronto, Canada
Area: 2.5 acres (1 hectare)
Completion date: 2012
Landscape design: Janet Rosenberg & Studio Landscape Architects
Photography: City of Toronto, Janet Rosenberg & Studio
Client: City of Toronto, Toronto Community Housing Corporation

Developed in partnership with the City of Toronto and Toronto Community Housing Corporation, Joel Weeks Park showcases excellence in design team collaboration, community consultation, and the coming together of a community. It has become the centerpiece of the regeneration of a neighborhood and pays homage to the history and geography of the area.

Joel Weeks Park expands on the former smaller Joel Weeks Parkette and provides critical open and flexible green space for the vibrant mixed-income Rivertowne community. It was designed to improve the quality of life of neighborhood residents, and to foster a sense of pride, ownership, and spirit of place for the community. The new park offers a central gathering area and community space, garden plots, multifunction sports court, bosque of birch trees, large grassy berms, children's play area, and an urban "river" element that includes a bridge that wraps around a water play area with jets.

Stormwater management takes advantage of the site's varied topography to direct water flow to a number of surface drains. The system uses city infrastructure to avoid standing water, and sheet flow across the hardscape and a dry swale in the perimeter of the playground provide an opportunity for children to play with moving water. On most days this is simply the collection of water discharged by water jets in the splash pad area of the playground.

① Common garden
② Water area
③ Play area
④ Basketball court

Site plan

1 Trees screen the entrance of the park
2 Entrance of the park has a sense of flow with curved planter edges

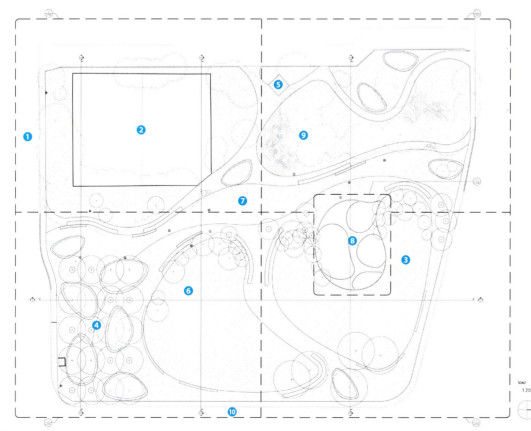

1 Thompson Street
2 Multi-functional courts
3 Grass mound
4 Tree grove
5 Existing building
6 Grass mound
7 Market area
8 Waterplay area
9 Grass mound
10 Munro Street

Zone plan

1 Young birch trees will grow to define a sense of enclosure along the
   urban edge of the park
2 Adaptable and colorful play elements encourage children to learn
   and discover

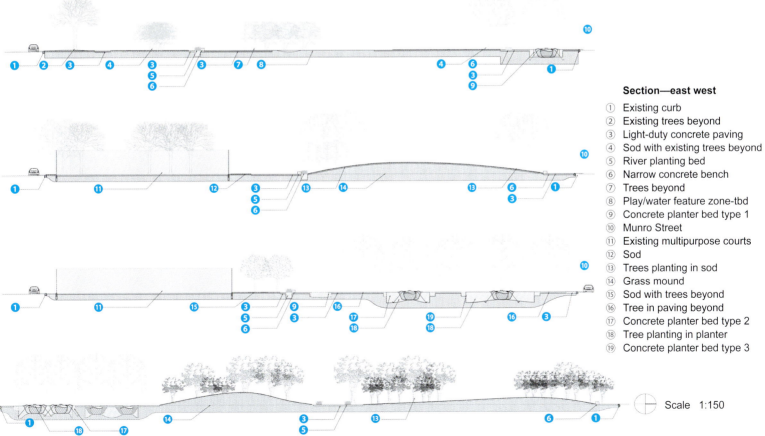

Section—east west

① Existing curb
② Existing trees beyond
③ Light-duty concrete paving
④ Sod with existing trees beyond
⑤ River planting bed
⑥ Narrow concrete bench
⑦ Trees beyond
⑧ Play/water feature zone-tbd
⑨ Concrete planter bed type 1
⑩ Munro Street
⑪ Existing multipurpose courts
⑫ Sod
⑬ Trees planting in sod
⑭ Grass mound
⑮ Sod with trees beyond
⑯ Tree in paving beyond
⑰ Concrete planter bed type 2
⑱ Tree planting in planter
⑲ Concrete planter bed type 3

Scale 1:150

Preliminary zone plan

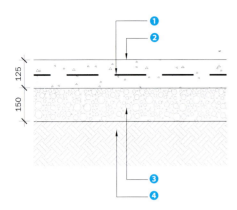

Light-duty concrete paving   Scale: 1:10

① Welded wire mesh
② Poured concrete slope for drainage
③ Granular type "A"
④ Compacted subgrade

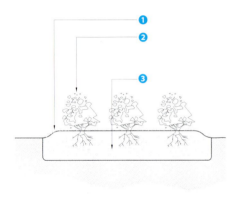

Herbacious planting   Scale: 1:10

① Continuous planting bed
② Herbacious plant
③ Planting soil mixtures as per specifications

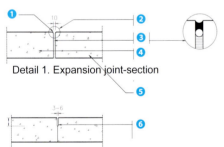

Detail 1. Expansion joint-section

Detail 2. Sawcut control joint-section

Detail 3. Tool edge finish-section

Control expansion joints   Scale: 1:10

① Rounded chamfer
② Joint sealant
③ Sealant/backer rod/pre-formed joint filler
④ Concrete paving, curb, walls
⑤ Concrete
⑥ Sawcut joint
⑦ Rounded chamfer on edges

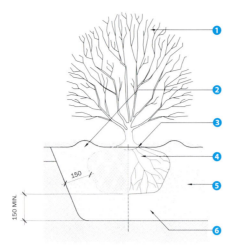

Shrub planting

① Prune to preserve the natural character of the plant
② For shrubs greater than 50 in (125 cm) HT. provide 4 in (10 cm) HT. saucer
③ Mulching—4-in (10-cm) depth mulch
④ Cut and remove burlap from top 1/3 of root ball or cut slit in organic container and remove bottom
⑤ Planting soil mixture as per specifications
⑥ Scarify surface of subsoil prior to planting

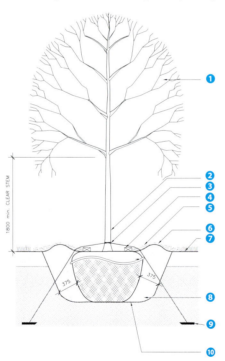

Tree planting in sod

① Prune only dead, broken, and crossing branches. Never remove more than 1/3 of the tree's canopy
② Caliper measured 1 ft (30 cm) above grade
③ Rope tie
④ 2' x 4' pressure treated lumber
⑤ Mulching—3 in (8 cm) depth mulch shredded pine or cedar
⑥ Provide 4 in (10 cm) HT. saucer
⑦ Cut, loosen, and remove top 1/3 of wire basket and burlap surrounding root ball
⑧ Backfill with planting soil mixture as per specifications. Tamp soil to eliminate air pockets and reduce settlement
⑨ "Duck ball" earth anchor root ball system
⑩ Scarify surface of subsoil prior to planting

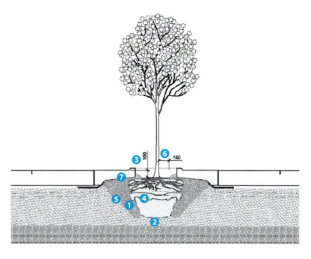

Tree planting in pavement

① Excavate planting hole, hand digging only
② Place root ball on undisturbed or compacted soil
③ Plant tree so top of the root ball is no more than 4 in (10 cm) below sidewalk
④ Cut, loosen, and roll back approx 1/2 of twine, burlap, and wire on root ball
⑤ Backfill with native soil in 6-in (15-cm) lifts and tamp to prevent air pockets
⑥ After water has been absorbed, cover with layer of mulch before installing precast planter covers. Add mulch as shown, keep mulch 6 in (15 cm) away from tree stem
⑦ Remove wrap from trunk and inspect for damage

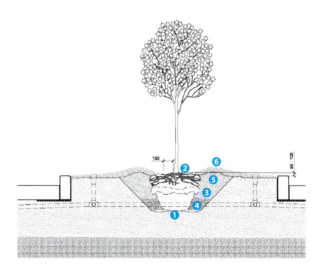

Tree planting in concrete planter

① Place root ball on undisturbed or compacted soil
② Plant tree so top of the root ball is 2–4 in (5–10 cm) above top of planter curb
③ Backfill with native soil in 6 in (15 cm) lifts and tamp to prevent air pockets
④ Backfill and compact the first 2 lifts firmly with feet to stabilize root ball
⑤ When 2/3 of depth of planting pit has been backfilled, fill remaining space with water. Once water has penetrated soil, backfill to finish garden
⑥ After water has been absorbed, cover with 4 in (10 cm) of mulch tapered to ground level at the trunk, keep mulch 6 in (15 cm) from trunk

1 Planting choices are intended to evoke a sense of flow and movement. Choices were
required to be hardy by necessity, and include grasses such as Calamagrostis, Miscanthus,
and Penisetum, and groundcover such as Siberian iris, daylily, ostrich fern, hosta, and
meadow sage
2 'Knockout Red Rose' is both hardy and a public favorite

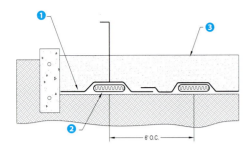

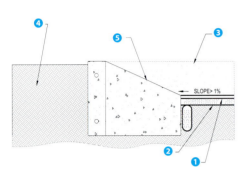

FibarSystem surface

① FibarFelt
② FibarDrain
③ Fibar® Engineered Wood Fibers
④ Accessible concrete ramp
⑤ Edge of ramp must comply with ASTM fall zone

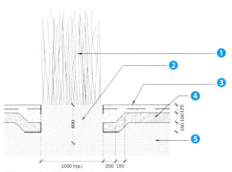

River planting bed

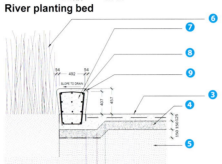

Concrete bench

① Herbaceous planting
② Planting soil
③ Light duty concrete
④ Granular type "A"
⑤ Compacted subgrade
⑥ River planting bed
⑦ Reinforced concrete bench to be coordinated with structural
⑧ Concrete with architectural finish
⑨ Skateboard deterrent

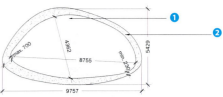

Concrete planter type 1

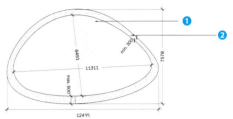

Concrete planter type 2

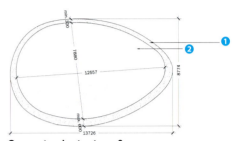

Concrete planter type 3

① Sod or planting
② Concrete paving

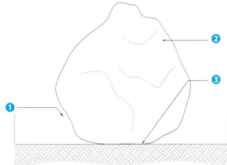

Boulder in FibarSystem surface

Log in FibarSystem surface

① FibarSystem surface
② Boulder to be supplied by contractor
③ Boulder to be installed and balanced to base of FibarSystem surface
④ Log to be supplied by contractor
⑤ Log to be cut at base and installed to base of FibarSystem surface

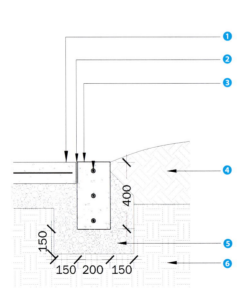

Flush concrete curb

① Light duty concrete
② Expansion joint
③ Concrete curb
④ Sod or FibarSystem surface
⑤ Granular type "A"
⑥ Compacted subgrade

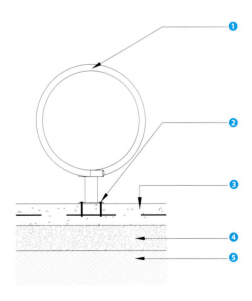

Helix 6-bike rack

① Helix 6-bike rack install as per manufacturer specifications
② Concrete spike supplied by manufacturer
③ Light duty concrete
④ Granular type "A"
⑤ Compacted subgrade

1-2 Elliptical planters provide large areas of loose soil while also being instrumental in generating a sense of flow through the site
3 Grass mounds offer not only a public prerequisite in lawn, but also the opportunity for play in winter, as well as a vertical element to screen and frame new construction. Pin oaks and Kentucky coffee trees are in addition to Betula nigra (Birch) and Trembling aspen

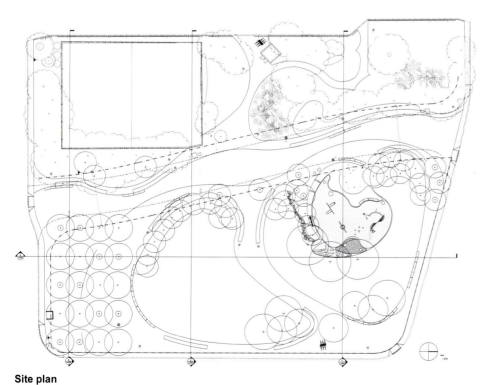

Site plan

- ○ Existing deciduous tree
- ✳ Existing coniferous tree
- ◎ New tree in paving
- ⊙ New tree
- ⬚ Tree protection zone
- ▢ Sod
- ▨ Fibar
- ▨ Sand
- ▦ Structural soil
- ▢ Concrete paving type 1
- ▢ Concrete paving type 2
- ▨ Concrete paving type 3
- ▢ Limestone slab
- ▢ Planting bed
- ◖ Concrete planter bed
- ◖ Concrete pea gravel bed
- ● Proposed light standard
- ▥ Catch basin
- ◉ Manhole
- ▧ Garbage receptacle
- —— Saw cut
- —— Expansion joint
- —·—· "Old" Carroll Street
- —··— Limit of work
- ----- Property line

1-2 Kentucky coffee trees placed around the perimeter of the playground will provide cover and shade for children. Trembling aspen adds to the theme of flow and movement. Combining the climbing and water elements in one area aids monitoring and safety of children

3-4 Scale of grasses offers children a lesson on the changing relationship between size and age

5 'Knockout Red Roses' were added as public favorites. Public art was integrated into the park

6 Water channels carry standing water away from the splash pad, while at the same time providing concentrated and visible flows before the water disappears at surface drains

Linear Park of Raycom City

Location: Hefei, China
Area: 123.5 acres (50 hectares)
Completion date: 2016
Landscape design: SWA Marco Esposito and Chih-Wei G.V. Chang
Photography: Tom Fox
Client: Raycom Real Estate Development Co., Ltd.

The new linear park in Raycom City provides a comfortable and convenient walking spine connecting the area's eight neighborhoods, various facilities, amenities, and transport.

Landscape architects SWA took inspiration from Hefei's river city identity to create a dynamic outdoor environment for the local residents who live in more than 100 neighborhood towers and spend a high percentage of their time in the area. The site is generally flat with row crops and a variety of outdoor spaces shaded by canopy trees.

The green space strives to provide the ultimate in sustainability. It is sculpted to capture on-site rainwater flows and has a waterway and series of rain gardens in lieu of storm pipes. A central outdoor spine with adjusted street grades forms a single self-draining watershed that can slow and cleanse stormwater. The 2,559-feet (780-meters) waterway conveys all rainwater that falls on the eastern 80 percent of the green space and central public streets. Drainage from a portion of the podiums and roofs of adjacent neighborhood towers is also directed into the waterway via building drain pipes. The waterway includes four intermediate ponds formed by weirs, as well as a large receiving basin at the eastern lowland where a small outflow pipe slowly releases drainage into the municipal storm pipe when the water exceeds the ordinary water level. A larger overflow structure 3.28 feet (1 meter) above the outflow pipe responds to the heavy storm events. By setting the waterway flow line 6.56 feet (2 meters) below the adjacent street and walkway paving, the open waterway is able to serve the same function as the in-street storm pipe it replaces, and to accommodate at-grade bridges for walking and vehicle access.

Raycom City phases I, II, and III with linear park in the center

District plan

1 Bridge, pavilion, and terraces at Triangle park
2 Triangle park form the air
3 Narrow wooden bridge crosses the river in Triangle park

Phase 1 plan enlargement

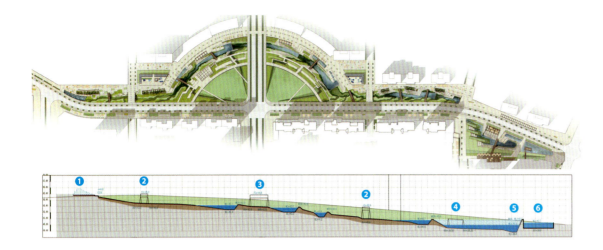

① Source Fountain Plaza
② Neighborhood access N-S road
③ Rain garden crossing Jinlu Road
④ Rain garden crossing Hutian Road
⑤ Triangle park retention pool
⑥ Triangle park lily pad

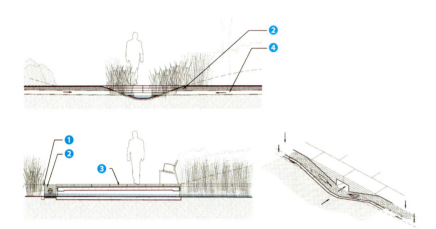

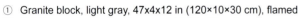

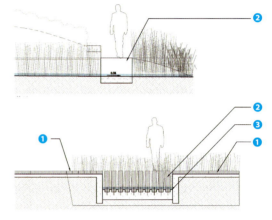

① Granite block, light gray, 47x4x12 in (120×10×30 cm), flamed
② Pebbles, various gray, size around 1.5 in (4 cm)
③ Granite block, warm beige, 47x23x3 in (120×60×7.5cm), flamed
④ Perf drain pipe, diameter 6 in (15 cm), with mitered drain cover

① Granite block, warm beige, 47x8x3 in (120×20×7.5cm), flamed
② Granite block, warm beige, 47x5x28 in (120×15×70cm), flamed
③ Top surface consistent with grading

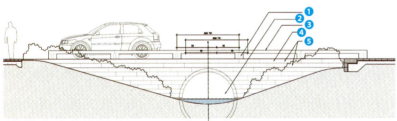

① Granite Lantern light,TYP., dark gray, 16x17x10 in (40x40×25 cm)
② Rain garden tunnel
③ Granite seat rail, dark gray, 118x20x6 in (300×50×15 cm), flamed top, cleft face
④ Granite block, dark gray, 47x24x8 in (120×60×20cm), flamed top, cleft face
⑤ Granite block, dark gray, 47x6x8 in (120×15×20cm), flamed top, cleft face

① Water source below stacked glass
② Fountain perimeter drain
③ Slot drain
④ Cut glass to edge abgle angle as shown
⑤ Tea pot

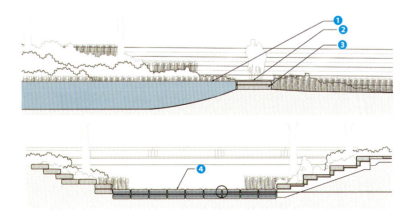

① Typical water level
② Granite block, warm beige, 47x24x8 in (120×60×20cm), cleft face and top
③ Mortar between granite block
④ Smoothly cleaved flamed top face and irregular cleft sides

1 Bridges across lush vegetation
2-3 Crescent park after rain
4 Water feature at stepped terrace

References and Resources

Introduction

Bolund, P., and Hunhammar, S. "Ecosystem Services in Urban Areas," *Ecological Economics* 29, (1999).

BOP Consulting. *Green Spaces: The Benefits for London*. London: City of London Corporation, 2013. Accessed January 2016. https://www.cityoflondon.gov.uk/business/economic-research-and-information/research-publications/Documents/research-2013/Green-Spaces-The-Benefits-for-London.pdf.

Abraham A., K. Sommerhalder, and T. Abel. "Landscape and Wellbeing: A Scoping Study on the Health-promoting Impact of Outdoor Environments," *International Journal of Public Health* 55, no. 1 (2010): 59–69.

Bowler, D., L. Buyung-Ali, T. Knight, and A. Pullin. "Urban Greening to Cool Towns and Cities: A Systematic Review of the Empirical Evidence," *Landscape and Urban Planning* 97 (2010): 147–155.

Byrne, Jason, and Neil Sipe. "Green and Open Space Planning for Urban Consolidation—A Review of the Literature and Best Practice." Brisbane: Griffith University, Urban Research Program, 2010.

Carr, S., M. Francis, L.G. Rivlin, and A. Stone. *Public Space*. New York: Cambridge University Press, 1992.

Chang, C.R., M.H. Li, and S.D. Chang. "A Preliminary Study on the Local Cool-island Intensity of Taipei City Parks," *Landscape and Urban Planning* 80, no. 4 (2007): 386–395.

Cities Alliance. Cities without Slums."World Statistics Day: A Look at Urbanization." 2010. Accessed April 2013. http://www.citiesalliance.org/node/2195.

City of London Corporation. *Open Spaces, 2012/13*. London: City of London Corporation, 2013. Accessed June 2013. http://content.yudu.com/Library/A27za5/OpenSpacesAnnualRepo/resources/index.htm?referrerUrl=http://free.yudu.com/item/details/952924/Open-Spaces-Annual-Report-2012.

Commission for Architecture and the Built Environment. *Open Space Strategies, Best Practice Guidance*. London: Commission for Architecture and the Built Environment and the Greater London Authority, 2009.

Coombes, E., A. Jones, and M. Hillsdon. "The Relationship of Physical Activity and Overweight to Objectively Measured Green Space Accessibility and Use," *Social Science and Medicine* 70, no. 6 (2010): 816–822.

Cooper-Marcus, Clare. *Design Guidelines: A Bridge Between Research and Decision-making*. Berkeley: Institute of Urban and Regional Development, University of California, 1995.

---. "The Needs of Children in Contemporary Cities." In *What We See: Advancing the Observations of Jane Jacobs*. Edited by Stephen Goldsmith and Lynne Elizabeth.Oakland, CA: New Village Press, 2010.

Cooper-Marcus, Clare, and Carolyn Francis, eds. *People Places: Design Guidelines for Urban Open Space*. Rev. 2nd ed. New York: John Wiley & Sons, 1998.

Cooper-Marcus, Clare, and Robin C. Moore. "Healthy Planet, Healthy Childhood: Designing Nature into the Daily Spaces of Childhood." In *Biophilic Design: The Theory, Science and Practice of Bringing Buildings to Life*. Edited by Stephen R. Kellert, Judith Heerwagen, and Martin Mador. New Jersey: John Wiley & Sons, 2008.

Cooper-Marcus, Clare, and Wendy Sarkissian. *Housing as if People Mattered: Illustrated Site-planning Guidelines for Medium-density Family Housing*. Berkeley: University of California Press, 1986.

Cushman & Wakefield. *European Cities Monitor, 2011*. Accessed April 2013. http://www.berlin-partner.de/fileadmin/user_upload/01_chefredaktion/02_pdf/studien-rankings/2011/Cushman%20&%20Wakefield%20-%20European%20Cities%20Monitor%20(2011%20english).pdf.

Cutt, H., B. Giles-Corti, L. Wood, M. Knuiman, and V. Burke. "Barriers and Motivators for Owners Walking." In *Spaces for Children: The Built Environment and Child Development*. Edited by C.S. Weinstein and T.G. David. New York: Plenum Press, 2008.

Dunnett, N., C. Swanwick, H. Woolley. *Improving Urban Parks, Play Areas and Green Spaces. Urban Research Paper*. London: Department for Transport, Local Government and the Regions, 2002.

Dunse, N., M. White, and C. Dehring. *Urban Parks, Open Space and Residential Property Values*. RICS Research Paper Series. London: RICS, 2007.

Ellaway, A., S. Macintyre, and X. Bonnefoy. "Graffiti, Greenery, and Obesity in Adults: Secondary Analysis of European Cross Sectional Survey," *British Medical Journal* 331, no. 7517 (2005): 611–612.

Esteban, A. *Natural Solutions. Nature's Role in Delivering Well-being and Key Policy Goals—Opportunities for the Third Sector*. London: New Economics Foundation, 2012. Accessed January 2016. http://b.3cdn.net/nefoundation/a39a39ba513ead1444_4gm6iszrq.pdf.

Findlay, Michael. "Social Housing for Culturally Diverse Groups: A Users' and Providers' Perspective." Unpublished PhD dissertation, University of Adelaide, School of Architecture, Landscape Architecture and Urban Design, March 2009.

Forest Research. *Benefits of Green Infrastructure. Report to Defra and CLG*. Farnham, UK: Forest Research, 2010. Accessed April 2013. http://www.forestry.gov.uk/pdf/urgp_benefits_of_green_infrastructure_main_report.pdf/$file/urgp_benefits_of_green_infrastructure_main_report.pdf.

Forsyth, Ann. *People and Urban Green Areas: Perception and Use. Design Brief Number 4*. Minneapolis, MN: Metropolitan Design Center, 2003.

Forsyth, Ann, and Laura Musacchio. *Designing Small Neighborhood Parks: A Manual for Addressing Social and Ecological Concerns*. New York: Wiley, 2005.

Francis, Carolyn, and Clare Cooper-Marcus. "Places People Take Their Problems." In *Healthy Environments: Proceedings of the 22nd Annual Conference of the Environmental Design Research Association (EDRA)*. Edited by J. Urbina-Soria, P. Ortega-Andeane, and R. Bechtel. Oklahoma City: EDRA, 1991.

---. "Restorative Places: Environment and Emotional Well-Being." In *Proceedings of the 23rd Annual Conference of the Environmental Design Research Association (EDRA)*. Oklahoma City: EDRA, 1992.

Fjørtoft, I., and J. Sageie. "The Natural Environment as a Playground for Children: Landscape Description and Analyses of a Natural Playscape," *Landscape and Urban Planning* 48 (2000): 83–97.

Luttik, J. "The Value of Trees, Water and Open Spaces as Reflected by House Prices in the Netherlands," *Landscape and Urban Planning* 48 (2000): 161.

Gehl Architects. *Public Spaces and Public Life*. Adelaide: City of Adelaide and Capital Cities Commission, Planning South Australia, 2002.

Gill, S.E., J.F. Handley, A.R. Ennos, and S. Pauleit. "Adapting Cities for Climate Change: the Role of the Green Infrastructure," *Built Environment* 33, no. 1 (2007): 115–133.

Gobster, P. ed. *Managing Urban and High-Use Recreation Settings*. St. Paul, MN: United States Department of Agriculture, North Central Forest Experiment Station, 1993.

Goličnik, Barbara, and Catharine Ward Thompson. "Emerging Relationships Between Design and Use of Urban Park Spaces," *Landscape and Urban Planning* 94 (2010): 38–53.

Grahn, P., and U.A. Stigsdotter. "Landscape Planning and Stress," *Urban Forestry & Urban Greening* 2, no. 1 (2003): 1–18.

GreenSpace. *The Park Life Report: The first ever public satisfaction survey of Britain's parks and green spaces*. Reading: GreenSpace, 2007.

Harnik, J. and B. Welle. *Measuring the Economic Value of a City Park System*. US: The Trust for Public Land, 2009.

Hutchinson, R. "Women and the Elderly in Chicago's Public Parks," *Leisure Sciences* 16 (1994): 229–247.

Jim, C. and W. Chen. "Assessing the Ecosystem Service of Air Pollutant Removal by Urban Trees in Guangzhou (China)," *Journal of Environmental Management* 88 (2008): 665–676.

Kaplan, R. "Nature at the Doorstep: Residential Satisfaction and the Nearby Environment," *Journal of Architectural and Planning Research* 2 (1985): 115–127.

---."The Nature of the View from Home: Psychological Benefits," *Environment and Behavior* 33, no. 4 (2001): 507–542.

Kaplan, R., and S. Kaplan. *The Experience of Nature: A Psychological Perspective*. Cambridge and New York: Cambridge University Press, 1989.

Kaplan, R., S. Kaplan, and R.L. Ryan. *With People in Mind: Design and Management of Everyday Nature*. Washington D.C.: Island Press, 1998.

Kaplan, S. "The Restorative Benefits of Nature: Toward an Integrative Framework," *Journal of Environmental Psychology* 15 (1995): 169–182.

Kellett, Jon, and Matthew W. Rofe. *Creating Active Communities: How Can Open and Public Spaces in Urban and Suburban Environments Support Active Living?* Adelaide: Active Living Coalition, 2009.

Kennedy, Rosemary. *Subtropical Design in South East Queensland: A Handbook for Planners, Developers and Decision-Makers*. Brisbane: Centre for Tropical Design, QUT, 2010.

Konijnendijk, C., M. Annerstedt, S. Maruthaveeran, and A. Nielsen. *Benefits of Urban Parks: A Systematic Review. A Report for IFPRA*. International Foundation of Parks and Recreation Administration, January 2013.

Kweon, B.S., W.C. Sullivan, and A.R. Wiley. "Green Common Spaces and the Social Interaction of Inner-city Older Adults," *Environment and Behavior* 30, no. 6 (1998): 832–858.

Lancaster, Jay. "Planning for the Dogs: Coopers Park." Unpublished essay, University of British Columbia, School of Community and Regional Planning, PLAN 548V, 15 August, 2007.

Land Use Consultants. *Making the Links: Greenspace and Quality of Life*. Scottish Natural Heritage Commissioned Report No. 060 (ROAME No. F03AB01), 2004.

Lee, A.C.K. and R. Maheswaran. "The Health Benefits of Urban Green Spaces: A Review of the Evidence," *Journal of Public Health* 33, no. 2 (2010): 212–222.

Lewis, C.A. "Effects of Plants and Gardening in Creating Interpersonal and Community Well-Being." In *Role of Horticulture in Human Well-being and Social Development: A National Symposium*. Edited by D. Relf. Arlington, VA: Timber Press, 1992.

Lewis, Charles A. *Green Nature/Human Nature: The Meaning of Plants in Our Lives*. Urbana and Chicago: University of Illinois Press, 1996.

Loukaitou-Sideris, A. "Urban Form and Social Context: Cultural Differentiation in the Uses of Urban Parks," *Journal of Planning Education and Research* 14 (1995): 89–102.

Louv, R. *Last Child in the Woods: Saving Our Children from Nature-Deficit Disorder*. Chapel Hill, NC: Algonquin Books, 2005.

Low, Setha M., Dana Taplin, and Suzanne Scheld. *Rethinking Urban Parks: Lessons in Culture and Diversity*. Austin: University of Texas Press, 2005.

Low, Setha M., Dana Taplin, Suzanne Scheld, and T. Fisher. "Recapturing Erased Histories: Ethnicity, Park Design and Cultural Representation," *Journal of Architectural and Planning Research* 19, no. 4 (2002): 131–148.

Lynch, K., ed. *Growing Up in Cities: Studies of the Spatial Environment of Adolescence in Cracow, Melbourne, Mexico City, Salta, Toluca and Warszawa*. Cambridge, MA: MIT Press, 1997.

Maas J., R.A. Verheij, P.P. Groenewegen, P. Spreeuwenberg, S. de Vries. "Physical Activity as a Possible Mechanism Behind the Relationship Between Green Space and Health: A Multilevel Analysis," *BMS Public Health* 8 (2008): 206.

Maeer, G., G. Fawcett, and T. Killick. *Values and Benefits of Heritage. A Research Review*. UK: Heritage Lottery Fund, 2012.

Maller, Cecily, and Mardie Townsend. "Children's Mental Health and Wellbeing and Hands-on Contact with Nature," *International Journal of Learning* 12, no. 4 (2006): 359–372.

Maller, Cecily J., Claire Henderson-Wilson, and Mardie Townsend. "Rediscovering Nature in Everyday Settings: Or How to Create Healthy Environments and Healthy People," *EcoHealth* 6, no. 4 (2009): 553–556.

Maller, Cecily, Mardie Townsend, Peter Brown, and Lawrence St Leger. *Healthy Parks Healthy People: The Health Benefits of Contact with Nature in a Park Context, A Review of the Current Literature*. Melbourne: Parks Victoria and Deakin University, Faculty of Behavioral Science, 2002.

Malone, K. *Every Experience Matters: An Evidence Based Research Report on the Role of Learning Outside the Classroom for Children's Whole Development from Birth to Eighteen Years.* Wollongong, Australia: Farming and Countryside Education for UK Department Children, School and Families, 2008.

Mercer. *2012 Quality of Living Worldwide City Ranking—Mercer Survey.*

Miller, K.F. *Designs on the Public: The Private Lives of New York's Public Spaces.* Minneapolis: University of Minnesota Press, 2007.

Mitchell, R., and F. Popham. "Effect of Exposure to Natural Environment on Health Inequalities: An Observational Population Study," *The Lancet* 372, no. 9650 (2008): 1655–1660.

Musacchio, L.R., and J. Wu. "Cities of Resilience: Integrating Ecology into Urban Design, Planning, Policy and Management." In *Proceedings of the 87th Annual Meeting of the Ecological Society of America/14th Annual Conference of the Society for Ecological Restoration.* Washington, D.C.: Ecological Society of America, 2002.

Mytton, O., N. Townsend, H. Rutter, and C. Foster. "Green Space and Physical Activity: an Observational Study Using Health Survey for England Data," *Health & Place* 18, no. 5 (2012): 1034–1041.

Natural England. *Monitor of Engagement with the Natural Environment Survey (2009–2012): Analysis of Data Related to Visits with Children.* Natural England, 2012. Accessed April 2013. http://publications.naturalengland.org.uk/publication/4654618.

New Zealand Ministry of Justice. *National Guidelines for Crime Prevention through Environmental Design in New Zealand.* Wellington: Ministry of Justice, 2005.

North Carolina State University, College of Design, Center for Universal Design. *The Principles of Universal Design.* Raleigh: North Carolina State University, 1997.

Nowak, D.J. *Air Pollution Removal by Chicago's Urban Forest, Chicago's Urban Forest Ecosystem: Results of the Chicago Urban Forest Climate Project.* United States Department of Agriculture, 1994.

NSW Department of Planning, Urban Design Advisory Service (UDAS). *Urban Design Guidelines with Young People in Mind.* Sydney: UDAS, 1998.

Owens, Patsy Eubanks, and Innisfree McKinnon. "In Pursuit of Nature: The Role of Nature in Adolescents' Lives," *Journal of Developmental Processes* 4, no. 1 (2009): 43–58.

Peiser, R.B., and G.M. Schwann. "The Private Value of Public Open Space within Subdivisions," *Journal of Architectural and Planning Research* 10, no. 2 (1993): 91-104.

Platt, R., R. Rowntree, and P. Muick, eds. *The Ecological City: Preserving and Restoring Biodiversity.* Amherst: University of Massachusetts Press, 1994.

Read, D.J., P.H. Freer-Smith, J.I.L. Morison, N. Hanley, C.C. West, and P. Snowdon, eds. *Combating Climate Change–A Role for UK Forests.* Edinburgh, UK: The Stationery Office, 2009.

Redland City Council. *Draft Open Space Strategy.* Unpublished report. Cleveland: Redland City Council, 2011.

Richardson, D., and M. Parker. *A Rapid Review of the Evidence Base in Relation to Physical Activity and Green Space and Health.* UK: HM Partnerships, NHS Ashton, Leigh and Wigan, 2011.

Sarkissian Associates Planners. *MirvacFini: Social Design Advice for High-density Housing Development.* The Peninsula, Perth, 2002–2003.

---. *Social Issues and Trends Associated with Medium to High Density Housing: Final Report for the Land Management Council.* Brisbane: Sarkissian Associates Planners, 2004.

Sarkissian, Wendy, Rebecca Bateman, and Brendan Hurley, with Andrea Young. *Open Space in Medium-density Housing Guidelines for Planning and Design.* September 2013. Accessed January 2016. http://www.sarkissian.com.au/wp-content/uploads/2013/09/Open-Space-in-Medium-Density-Neighbourhoods-web.pdf.

Sarkissian, Wendy, and Graeme Dunstan. "Stories in a Park: Reducing Crime and Stigma through Community Storytelling," *Urban Design Forum Quarterly* 64, no. 12 (2013).

Sarkissian, Wendy, and Kristin Stewart. *ACT Crime Prevention and Urban Design: Resource Manual.* Canberra: ACT Government, Urban Services, 2000.

Sarkissian, Wendy, Steph Walton, Helen Kerr, Angela Hazebroek, Elyssa Ludher, and Saville, Gregory. *Safe Growth: A New Way Forward, Strands that Bind Neighborhood Participation, CPTED and Community Development.* Alter Nation, Inc., 2007.

Shah, H., and J. Peck. *Well-being and the Environment–Achieving 'One Planet Living' and Maintaining Quality of Life.* London: New Economics Foundation, 2005.

Seeland, K., S. Dübendorfer, and R. Hansmann. "Making Friends in Zurich's Urban Forests and Parks: The Role of Public Green Space for Social Inclusion of Youths from Different Cultures," *Forest Policy and Economics* 11 (2009): 10–17.

Smith, D. *Valuing Housing and Green Spaces: Understanding Local Amenities, the Built Environment and House Prices in London (GLA Working Paper 42).* Greater London Authority, 2010.

Simmons, D.A. "Urban Children's Preferences for Nature: Lessons for Environmental Education," *Children's Environments* 11, no. 3 (1994): 194-203.

State of Queensland. Queensland Government. *Crime Prevention Through Environmental Design, Guidelines for Queensland, Part A.* Brisbane: Queensland State Government, 2007.

---. *Crime Prevention Through Environmental Design, Guidelines for Queensland, Part B.* Brisbane: Queensland State Government, 2007.

---. *The Sustainable Planning Act 2009.* Brisbane: Queensland State Government, 2009.

State of Queensland. Queensland Government. Department of Infrastructure, Local Government and Planning. *Statutory Guideline Priority Infrastructure Plans, A Guideline for the Preparation of Priority Infrastructure Plans under the Sustainable Planning Act 2009.* Brisbane: State of Queensland, Department of Local Government and Planning, 2011.

State of Queensland. Queensland Government. Department of State Development. *Next Generation Planning, Affordable Living Smart Growth Form-based Codes SEQ Place Model, A Handbook for Planners, Designers and Developers in South East Queensland.* Brisbane: Council of Mayors (SEQ), 2011.

---."Livable Compact Cities Project LCCP." Unpublished report. Brisbane: Council of Mayors (SEQ), 2011.

Sustainable Development Commission. *Health, Place and Nature: How Outdoor Environments Influence Health and Well-being: A Knowledge Base.* Sustainable Development Commission, 2008.

Swanwick, C., and H. Woolley. *Improving Urban Parks, Play Areas and Green Spaces.* London: Department for Transport, Local Government and the Regions, 2002. Accessed April 2013. http://www.ocs.polito.it/biblioteca/verde/improving_full.pdf.

Talen, Emily. "The Spatial Logic of Parks," *Journal of Urban Design* 15, no. 4 (2010): 473–491.

Tapley, B., P. Settles, and R. Brooke. *Sustainability Assessment of Global Financial Centers.* London: City of London, 2008.

Taylor, A.F., F.E. Kuo, and W.C. Sullivan. "Views of Nature and Self-discipline: Evidence from Inner City Children," *Journal of Environmental Psychology* 11, no. 1-2 (2002): 49–63.

Tinsley, H.A., D.J. Tinsley, and C.E. Croskeys. "Park Usage, Social Milieu and Psychosocial Benefits of Park Use Reported by Older Urban Park Users from Four Ethnic Groups," *Leisure Sciences* 24 (2002): 199–218.

Tiwary, A., D. Sinnett, C.J. Peachey, Z. Chalabi, S. Vardoulakis, T. Fletcher, G. Leonardi, C. Grundy, A. Azapagic, and T.R. Hutchings. "An Integrated Tool to Assess the Role of New Planting in PM10 Capture and the Human Health Benefits: A Case Study in London," *Environmental Pollution* 157, (2009): 2645–2653.

TNS Travel and Tourism. *London Visitor Survey Annual Report 2008 January—December.* London Development Agency, 2008.

Tzoulas, K., K. Korpela, S. Venn, V. Yli-Pelkonen, A. Kazmierczak, J. Niemela, and P. James. "Promoting Ecosystem and Human Health in Urban Areas Using Green Infrastructure: A Literature Review," *Landscape and Urban Planning* 81 (2007): 167–178.

UN-HABITAT. *Cities and Climate Change: Global Report on Human Settlements 2011.* London: Earthscan, 2011.

United Nations. Department of Economic and Social Affairs, Population Division. *World Urbanization Prospects: The 2005 Revision. Working Paper No. ESA/P/WP/2006.* Accessed April 2013. http://www.un.org/esa/population/publications/WUP2005/2005WUP_FS7.pdf.

Urban Land Development Authority. *Park Planning and Design, ULDA Guideline No. 12.* Brisbane: Urban Land Development Authority, 2011.

USDA Forest Service. "Trees For Children: Helping Inner City Children Get a Better Start in Life," *Technology Bulletin*, no. 7 (2001).

Van den Berg, A., J. Maas, R. Verheij, and P. Groenewegen. "Green Space as a Buffer Between Stressful Life Events and Health," *Social Science & Medicine* 70 (2010): 1203–1210.

Van Herzele, A., and S. de Vries. "Linking Green Space to Health: A Comparative Study of Two Urban Neighborhoods in Ghent, Belgium," *Population and Environment* 34, no. 2 (2012): 171–193.

White, M., I. Alcock, B. Wheeler, and M. Depledge. *Would You Be Happier Living in a Greener Urban Area? A Fixed Effects Analysis of Panel Data.* European Center for Environment and Human Health, 2013.

White, Rob. "Public Spaces, Consumption and the Social Regulation of Young People." In *Youth, Globalization and the Law.* Edited by S.A. Venkatesh and R. Kassimir. Palo Alto, California: Stanford University Press, 2007.

---. "Youth Participation in Designing Public Space," *Youth Studies Australia* 20, no. 1 (2001): 19–26.

Whitzman, Carolyn. *The Handbook of Community Safety Gender and Violence Prevention.* London: Earthscan, 2008.

Woolley, H., and S. Rose. *The Value of Public Space. How High Quality Parks and Public Spaces Create Economic, Social and Environmental Value.* CABE Space, 2004. Accessed April 2013. http://webarchive.nationalarchives.gov.uk/20110118095356/http:/www.cabe.org.uk/publications/the-value-of-public-space.

Yu, C., and W. Hien. "Thermal Benefits of City Parks," *Energy and Buildings* 38 (2006): 105–120.

Zhang, B., G. Xie, C. Zhang, and J. Zhang. "The Economic Benefits of Rainwater Runoff Reduction by Urban Green Spaces: A Case Study in Beijing, China," *Journal of Environmental Management* 100 (2012): 65–71.

Green Space and Stormwater Management Practice

Livingston, Eric H., and Ellen McCarron. *Stormwater Management: A Guide for Floridians.* Florida Department of Environmental Regulation, 1991. Accessed January 2016. http://www.dep.state.fl.us/water/nonpoint/docs/nonpoint/Stormwater_Guide.pdf.

Goettemoeller, Robert L., and David P. Hansellmann. *Ohio Stormwater Control Guidebook.* Columbus, Ohio: Ohio Department of Natural Resources, Division of Soil and Water Conservation, 1980.

Hyde, Luther. *Principal Aquifers in Florida.* Florida: Florida Bureau of Geology, 1975.

Livingston, Eric H., Ellen McCarron, John Cox, and Patricia Sanzone. *The Florida Development Manual: A Guide to Sound Land and Water Management.* Nonpoint Source Management Section. Florida Department of Environmental Regulation, 1988. Accessed January 2016. https://www.swfwmd.state.fl.us/files/database/site_file_sets/1959/FL_Devel_Ch6-Sec310.pdf.

North Carolina Division of Coastal Management. *A Guide to Protecting Coastal Waters Through Local Planning.* Raleigh, N.C.: North Carolina Department of Natural Resources and Community Development, Division of Coastal Management, 1986.

Schueler, Thomas R. *Controlling Urban Runoff, A Practical Manual for Planning and Designing Urban BMPs.* Washington, D.C.: Metropolitan Washington Council of Governments, 1987.

State of Queensland. Queensland Government. Department of Infrastructure and Planning. *South East Queensland Regional Plan 2009–2031, Implementation Guideline No. 7 Water Sensitive Urban Design–Design Objectives for Urban Stormwater Management.* Brisbane: Queensland Government, 2009.

Design Guidelines for Green Space in the Community

County of Los Angeles. Department of Parks and Recreation. *Planning and Development Agency. Park Design Guidelines and Standards.* June 2014. Accessed January 2016. http://file.lacounty.gov/dpr/cms1_216063. pdf.

ASTM International. *Standard Consumer Safety Performance Specification for Playground Equipment for Public Use. Active Standard ASTM F1487.* Accessed January 2016. http://www.astm.org/Standards/F1487.htm.

Atlas, Randall. *21st Century Security and CPTED: Designing for Critical Infrastructure Protection and Crime Prevention.* Florida: CRC Press, 2008.

California Invasive Plant Council (Cal-IPC). Accessed January 2016. http://www.cal-ipc.org/.

California Weed Science Society (CWSS). Accessed January 2016. http://www.cwss.org/.

County of Los Angeles. Department of Public Works. *Low Impact Development Standards Manual February 2014.* Accessed January 2016. https://dpw.lacounty.gov/ldd/lib/fp/Hydrology/Low%20Impact%20Development%20Standards%20Manual.pdf.

---."Watershed Management Division." Accessed January 2016. http://www.dpw.lacounty.gov/wmd/.

Crowe, Timothy. *Crime Prevention Through Environmental Design.* 2nd ed. USA: Butterworth-Heinemann, 2000.

Grattan, S., C. Grieve, A. Harivandi, L. Rollins, D. Shaw, B. Sheikh, K. Tanji, and L. Wu. *Salt Management Guide for Landscape Irrigation with Recycled Water in Coastal Southern California: A Comprehensive Literature Review.* Accessed January 2016. http://www.salinitymanagement. org/Literature_Review.pdf.

Los Angeles County. *Department of Regional Planning. Green Building and Sustainability Guidelines for the County of Los Angeles 2008 Edition.* http://planning. lacounty.gov/green.

Sustainable Sites Initiative. "The Sustainable Sites Initiative." Accessed January 2016. http://www. sustainablesites.org/.

U.S. Consumer Product Safety Commission. *Handbook for Public Playground Safety.* Bethesda, MD:U.S. Consumer Product Safety Commission, 2015. Accessed January 2016. https://www.cpsc.gov//PageFiles/122149/325.pdf.

U.S. Green Building Council. Accessed January 2016. http://www.usgbc.org/DisplayPage.aspx?CategoryID=19.

Weed Research and Information Center. Accessed January 2016. http://wric.ucdavis.edu/.

Weed Science Society of America. Accessed January 2016. http://www.wssa.net/.

Western Society of Weed Science. Accessed January 2016. http://www.wsweedscience.org/.

Index

Published in Australia in 2016 by
The Images Publishing Group Pty Ltd
Shanghai Office
ABN 89 059 734 431
6 Bastow Place, Mulgrave, Victoria 3170, Australia
Tel: +61 3 9561 5544 Fax: +61 3 9561 4860
books@imagespublishing.com
www.imagespublishing.com

Copyright © The Images Publishing Group Pty Ltd 2016
The Images Publishing Group Reference Number: 1267

Title: Green Space in the Community / edited by Steffan Robel.
ISBN: 9781864706536

For Catalogue-in-Publication data, please see the National Library of Australia entry

Printed by Everbest Printing (Guangzhou) Co Ltd., in China

IMAGES has included on its website a page for special notices in relation to this and our other publications. Please visit www.imagespublishing.com.